Praise for *Sex Bomb*:

'Honest. Much needed. I was surprised several times'
– **Frank Skinner**

'*Sex Bomb* is so hilarious, raw and poignant.
I couldn't put it down!'
– **Jena Friedman**

'A hilarious, courageous and compelling read that
explores the complicated relationship between
culture, religion, identity and sexuality within the
British Asian community. A must read for those
who have lived it, and for those who haven't'
– **Anita Bhagwandas**

'Azmat raises complex, consequential matters with
a lightness of touch. *Sex Bomb* is an easy read as she
reflects candidly and boldly on her experiences
and the factors that led to them'
– *Chortle*

'*Sex Bomb* is a privilege and a joy to read,
and everybody you've ever met should read it'
– **Anne T. Donahue**

'Refreshing, candid, hilarious and necessary'
– **Sarah Malik**

Sadia Azmat is a British Asian stand-up comedian and writer from East London. Through a chance encounter with a comedian in a call centre, she was introduced to the circuit, and now she is a regular stand-up. In 2018 Sadia launched her critically acclaimed BBC podcast 'No Country For Young Women' which was named as one of the 'Best audio 2018' by the *Observer* and Apple's Top picks for 2018. *Sex Bomb* is her first book.

Sex Bomb

The Life and Loves of an Asian Babe

SADIA AZMAT

HEADLINE

First published in 2022 by
HEADLINE PUBLISHING GROUP

First published in paperback in 2023 by
HEADLINE PUBLISHING GROUP

1

Cataloguing in Publication Data is available from the British Library

ISBN: 978 1 4722 8581 2

Typeset in Berling by CC Book Production

Printed and bound in Great Britain by Clays Ltd, Elcograf S.p.A.

Cover design by Anna Morrison

Commissioning Editor: Katie Packer
Developmental Edit: Sarah Shaffi
Copy-editor: Aruna Vasudevan
Proofreader: Jill Cole

Song lyric credit: 'Mad About the Boy' by Noël Coward, on Pg 60;
and 'Black' by Dave, on Pg 217

Headline's policy is to use papers that are natural, renewable and
recyclable products and made from wood grown in well-managed forests
and other controlled sources. The logging and manufacturing processes
are expected to conform to the environmental regulations
of the country of origin.

HEADLINE PUBLISHING GROUP
An Hachette UK Company
Carmelite House
50 Victoria Embankment
London EC4Y 0DZ

www.headline.co.uk
www.hachette.co.uk

For Nadeem

Contents

Prologue

Once,* when I pulled the short straw, my mum asked me to go to the newsagents to do the shopping and pick up the usual – some pitta bread, milk and butter. I was about eight years old and tried to avoid boring chores whenever I could, but my parents were conscious of instilling responsibility in me as early as possible. There was always a sense we were on borrowed time and they didn't want to encourage complacency.

---

* White people, I know you love asking questions, so I've created footnotes just for you. Everyone else feel free to skip past these. Also white people, please note, this is not a book about Islam, so please refer to the official stuff if you're interested.

I had thrown on a white T-shirt and blue shorts and hunched my shoulders in defeat as I walked down the road to the local shop. I was easily distracted by the goodies when I got there. I would always take my time scoping out all the shelves and looking at the ice creams through the freezer door, my fingers hurting as I left them against the cold glass for too long.

Though I did many trips to the local shop, this time stands out to me, because on that day I saw an oldish white man in a suit flicking through the magazines section. On the top shelf, too high for me to reach, I noticed that the entire row was dedicated to pornographic magazines. I'd come across passing references to these on television before, but this was the first time I was ever confronted with them in real life. I was transfixed even though I knew I was not their intended audience: these magazines were for 'adults only'.

Magazine after glossy magazine showed women dolled up like they had an important engagement to attend to, except they can't have been going anywhere because they were all posing with their boobs out. My initial feeling was shock at the shopkeeper's negligence as I felt it was his responsibility to have shielded me from these explicit images. At the same time, I felt intrigued, and with the blame firmly off my shoulders, I kept gazing. All the magazines had white, blonde women on the front of them, except the one the man had picked up.

Prologue

The magazine in his hand was bright yellow and had the title *Asian Babes** written in capital letters across the top, in the same style as the bubble font used for Bollywood movie posters. It had three Asian women on the cover, with one looking distinctly Indian. I would have gasped but I knew this was something I should not have been looking at. I tried to safeguard my modesty by focusing on their faces rather than the rest of them. They were smiling and looked so happy.

This was two firsts for me, seeing Brown girls on the cover of a magazine and seeing them in compromising positions. I almost dropped the pitta bread.

Although I knew their semi-nudity was naughty, because that's what I'd been told, I did not know why. I didn't understand why, if it was wrong, they were being displayed in a shop in broad daylight. Yes, the magazines were out of reach, but they were definitely not out of sight.

Of course, the fact that these women were scantily dressed was an attraction for the men viewing them, but I also knew that the reason men lusted for these Asian women was because they couldn't have them. It was taboo. They were unattainable, part of a group that was forbidden for them to explore.

These guys were not only into Asian women, they

---

* British softcore pornographic magazine which featured photographs of women of South Asian, Korean, Chinese, Japanese and Thai origins.

were jerking off to us. That was very curious to me. I looked hard at the cover of the magazine and wondered what the women's parents thought or if they'd run away from home, but what I couldn't bring myself to consider at the time was that this was their choice, or that they might have enjoyed this work.

I didn't understand the position these women would hold in their families or communities. Once they'd put it all out there, could they be part of the same structures I was a part of, or did they have to sacrifice them for their work? I pondered on what motivated them to be photographed half-naked because up until then I'd been told all their special bits should be for one person. Was this giving back to society by sharing their special bits with the world, and by doing so were they still special? Were they from off the beaten track and, if so, could they simply return to the fold if they should choose to later down the line?

I had never seen Asian women depicted this way before and I almost felt betrayed. Until that point, I'd only seen Asian women cower in shyness if a man should even come as close as a metre towards them in Bollywood movies. I'd always been taught how innocent we were and what good homemakers we were. Suddenly I was seeing that Asian women could be a 'type' or sexually desirable, and that they could even be confident enough to show their bodies on a public platform. Obviously as a kid it's not usually that impressive seeing a woman with her bits out but because this was rare and unheard of it had a revolutionary impact on me.

At its peak in the nineties, *Asian Babes* was the highest grossing erotica magazine in the UK, which was no small feat considering such women were deemed 'repressed', 'conservative' and 'frigid'.

Standing in that local shop on that regular day was the first time I'd ever understood that I, Sadia Azmat, possessed sexuality. It made me feel awkward and funny but also a little naughty (in a good way). Up until then, it was all hidden and kept secret with a lack of knowledge but, in that moment, standing with the cover staring me in the face, there was nowhere to hide. I was confronted by sex bombs for the first time, and not only that, the consideration that a sex bomb could be an Asian babe like me. It opened up the possibility to me that, to my future partner, I could be one.

Though I may have become aware that I had sexuality, it didn't mean I had any idea what it meant or what to do with it.

And that's where this book comes in.

1

Cinderella

Growing up, the books I read taught me that when I got older Prince Charming* would come and save me if I was in trouble. I loved the happy endings in these stories and I took what my primary school teacher, Ms Clarke, said literally – that when it was my time the right man would turn up out of nowhere and rescue me.

At home and in the real world, however, I was taught that when I came of age, I would have to leave my family home to go and live with a husband (unlikely to be anything like the Prince Charming of

---

* Location is still unknown, possibly stuck in traffic. (Is it possible to report someone you've never met missing?)

my dreams) in something that's called an arranged marriage.*

As a kid, it was a very real prospect that my marriage might be negotiated at any given moment. Not in a child sex-trafficking sense, I might add. More that my parents were talent-scouting and assessing which families or empires they could infiltrate through marriage, sifting through the solid offers from the chancers.

I decided, rather than jump into the rabbit hole and start awkward conversations with my parents, to use less incriminating means to amass valuable insight into this sphere of love, marriage and relationships – which made me feel so blindsided. To learn more, I had to rely on clues mainly from overheard conversations, Bollywood movies and family case studies.† From all this, I started to gain a picture of what marriage and love might look like for me, and it wasn't always pretty.

I wasn't from a rich family, so it was likely the union wouldn't be a particularly celebratory affair when it happened. It felt so clinical to be marrying out of necessity or for sustenance. However, it might have been doable, if it weren't for my relatives in India who

---

* This seeded separation anxiety very early. Without having life experience to see that moving away from my family was a natural order of life, it made me feel an imbalanced and unwavering pull to stay in the family home.

† Combination of hearsay and examples from other family members.

would plot for the marriage to fail before it had even begun, if they didn't agree with the match.

People who were deemed 'underclass' often felt slighted by others who had the prospect to marry and move above their 'station'. To even get to the marriage part though, I had to be the best version of myself around men at all times, lest they were sizing me up as a potential bride. Anything I did that could be considered wrong might mean my options for a husband could diminish altogether and news travelled fast in my community, especially bad news. This added to the pressure of, not only living up to my parents, but my entire neighbourhood's expectations from a very young age.

My arranged marriage was often used as leverage if I was misbehaving, as my parents knew that I didn't want to settle down in India. School was my escapism from this, and in the end focusing on the books worked to my advantage. My parents saw me studying hard and gave me their blessing to focus on my education and career, instead of marriage, as they felt I had strong potential. Having taught me nothing about relationships and the opposite sex, I think they were also worried a man would run rings around me, which was almost prophetical in its accuracy. However, even though the consideration of arranged marriage stopped being a huge issue for me as I grew older and kept my head down, I had so many questions when it remained a real possibility for me, and this has continued throughout my life.

*Would I have to live with the husband and his parents for good?**

Could I be financially independent?

Why did I have to leave my family?

Why couldn't the guy come and stay with me?

Could I work? . . .

I couldn't discuss any of these things with my parents in case they mistook this curiosity for a change in heart. My parents had accepted that it wasn't a priority for me, for the time being, but I couldn't rely on the fact that my relatives in India wouldn't try and convince them to marry me off, or that they might suddenly decide education wasn't enough and that I would need a man. The threat of arranged marriage still hung over me and lingered for a long time. I was cautious therefore not to be good marriage material.

I stayed in my room a lot as a child out of a deep fear that my parents would invite a man around un-announced, who would take me away from my family and home. I even refused to learn how to make a cup of tea because it's a ritual for any bride-to-be to make tea for the husband-to-be and in-laws!

Most young girls, irrespective of their background,

---

* Bollywood movies showed brides moving in with their husbands. The expectation was for the husband to be your caregiver, and a woman moving away from her original family home to live with their in-laws was symbolic of this.

dream of their Big Day. I denied myself this pastime by distancing myself from anything remotely associated with marriage, just to ensure my parents did not get their hopes up. I remembered from reading *Cinderella* in class that no one wanted to marry the ugly sisters, so I modelled myself on them. I was fascinated by them. How did they stay single and free? They were flawed, and yet real because of that.

I rejected the pressures to conform to societal beauty standards and instead found contentment from food and not prescribing to accepted notions of femininity. I shied away from lipstick and pretty clothes, wanting to suppress my womanhood as long as possible, in the interests of stretching my freedom along with it.

Originally, I based my understanding of arranged marriages on what I saw on the screen in the world of Bollywood. A stallion of a man would emerge out of the gateways of heaven and fight hard to convince the woman's parents, who thought their daughter was too good for marriage, for their blessing. This suggested that marriage wasn't the best future for a woman, and so made me wary of it.

It was confusing to me that although the wedding was seen as the Big Day in most of these movies, everyone seemed happy but for the bride, who had an obligation to shed tears rather than celebrate. Since this was also the day when she would be losing her virginity, it gave the impression that this was something she was not happy about. The happy ever after was for the sake of everyone else, irrespective of what she wanted. It was a sacrifice.

We didn't use the term 'arranged marriage' at home, it was just marriage to us, however outside of our home and community, it was clearly a loaded term. When I got older, I learnt that some white people looked down on arranged marriages. They would get uncomfortable if the subject came up as it wasn't what they practised. They would often corner me into 'hypothetical scenarios' to find out where I stood. They'd pose the question, 'Would you rather have an arranged or a love marriage if you had to choose?' I hated when this happened because it put me in a difficult position, trying to explain and defend something I didn't fully understand myself, and that hadn't been explained to me, as well as it being patronising to me and my perspective.

It felt like they confused arranged marriage with forced marriage, which is basically where the bride, or occasionally both the bride and groom, are coerced into marriage. However, Islam is expressly against forced marriages. White people are just so put out by the mention of its existence that I think they wilfully misunderstand what arranged marriage means in real terms. I usually agreed with their exasperation, not wanting an arranged marriage myself, but felt a need to defend my culture from their prying eyes. Especially as I knew their understanding was more often than not surface level. I wasn't always sure whether their critique of arranged marriage was a smokescreen for the real issues they had with Asians. It was a good way of critiquing us while still 'keeping up appearances'.

The conversations I had with white people when I was younger and more naïve tended to be very predictable. I would always act like everything was perfect so they didn't think badly of the entire Asian race, and while white people appeared accepting of my standpoint I knew mostly they were holding back for fear of being considered anything but tolerant. Arranged marriage has always felt like a huge difference between us, despite it being a standard feature of white people's not so distant history too.

When I was eighteen years old, I learnt that the arranged part simply meant the couple didn't meet each other off their own backs: much like the European aristocracy, introductions were made through their families or matchmakers. (This made me thankful for not having any extended family in the UK as it made it more difficult to establish these arrangements long distance.) I didn't feel Islam required me to have an arranged marriage, without love, but given it is frowned upon for men and women to date before marriage, I wasn't quite sure what the alternative would be. Islam dictates that you use a wali*, who acts like a chaperone to assist with the selections and support the match-making process.

Ultimately, South Asian marriages are based on duty and fulfilling obligations towards one another. In some ways they place a greater weight on the marriage itself rather than the person that you marry. There is an expectation to hit the ground running and to be a good wife, however, there is no advice about how to have a successful marriage at all. There are just understandings you take with you, to serve your in-laws and 'keep the marriage' even when things get hard. If a wife dared to mention any challenges or fears, these would be quickly extinguished with some proverbs like: 'Patience is not about how long you can wait, but how well you behave while you're waiting.' This is all well and good, but it often provides no solution to the predicament.

I learnt the semantics and structures of relationships within my culture and communities, but this meant that actual relationships were a mystery to me. These ancient and rigid traditions are beautiful concepts but they have strayed so far from the real world that they serve more of a way to highlight failings as opposed to being a steady foundation upon which to form a relationship. I didn't know what partnership meant and though I'm sure a healthy relationship combined

---

* *Wali* means guardian or leader.

the practicalities with emotions, I wasn't allowed to acknowledge or act on the latter.

I couldn't get my head around the fact that I might not meet my intended partner, for all intents and purposes, until the wedding night. To me it seemed no different to a one-night stand, except with a lifetime worth of strings attached. Alongside this, a key component missing from the conversations around arranged marriage was what I could hope to get out of it outside of security and stability. A lot of the things you might gain were kept discreet, presumably to preserve the bride's modesty. The bride was supposed to simply trust the elders who apparently had her best interests at heart.

I'd heard the story of the Mughal emperor, Shah Jahan. He loved his wife Mumtaz Mahal so much that he had the Taj Mahal built in honour of her beauty after she passed away. I definitely felt a man should love a woman so much as to want to construct a building for her. But once the building was done, he had the hands of the workers chopped off, so they couldn't construct another monument as beautiful. That was crazy. I didn't want anyone to get hurt because of someone's love for me.

As this seventeenth-century tale was the only time I'd heard a woman receiving anything, it gave me the impression that I shouldn't expect much of anything. I guessed that my end of the bargain would be hassle from in-laws, room and board for which I'd trade a lifetime's worth of housework and maybe Sundays off. This left young girls aged five or six like me making very serious considerations about our fidelity and worth at a frightfully young age. As I saw how the women before me could be so passive in their own marriages, it left me unsure of what to look for in a relationship, could I even hope for looks, wealth or personality in my future life partner? In a hadith* it states the reasons people tend to marry are for wealth, lineage, beauty and religious commitment. Wealth I can get for sure (I'd like a Chanel purse just like any girl), but still all these reasons felt like they didn't dive deep enough into what makes two people want to be together *forever*, or provide enough reason for a woman to give half of herself and her whole commitment.

Although I was living in East London, the way my parents' generation interacted with one another was the same as if they were in their motherlands (India/ Pakistan). This meant I was subject to the same level of scrutiny as if I were living in a small Indian town. If anyone† so much as heard a rumour about me, like coming home late or being seen out with a boy, it was game over. My private affairs were anything but private

---

* Hadith are records of traditions or sayings of the Prophet Muhammad (peace and blessings upon him) PBUH.
† Community, neighbours, ill-meaning strangers.

and it was incumbent on me to declare (to prove) my sexual intentions were null and void. To even admit to having any sexual inclinations or desires was deplorable and so shameful that it was even worse than committing the act. It was 'sexual cleansing' where I had to be clear that I was clean and innocent and definitely not downright vulgar and mischievous.

For young women who did go ahead with traditional arranged marriages it sent a frightful, if realistic, message about her worth. That her virginity was a commodity and her biggest selling point. That her consent was diluted as it was also obtainable by proxy through her parents or guardians. That dissidence was punishable most likely by divorce and the excommunication of her from wider society.[*] I couldn't help but absorb how fundamental my virginity was to my identity, and so trying to contemplate who I would be without it frightened me. It meant I didn't form any self-worth growing up as no weight was placed on other characteristics like my sense of humour, intellect or aspirations. An arranged marriage was the only version of love that girls like me were taught – and there was no mention of what fate women who did not comply[†] faced. I had no other discourse on

---

[*] This was the best-case scenario, there were many instances of dissidence that were treated less lightly, particularly for women.

[†] Looks of pity and the stench of failure followed her around.

relationships growing up: it was arranged marriage or nothing.

It didn't matter that arranged marriages were happy ever after, as long as they were *ever* after. Divorce was taboo growing up, and although they have steadily increased in the Asian community, it remains that way today. No one ever talks about them or tries to take cautionary lessons. It's another reason why I resisted marriage, I couldn't ever see myself getting divorced because of how harshly women were judged for it and disregarded, so I continued to avoid men.

As you might expect, a man is able to get a divorce, known as a triple *talaq*, by saying 'I divorce you' three times to his wife. In Saudi Arabia, men are empowered to divorce women by simply sending a text message. For a woman, however, getting a divorce is a lengthier process and can only be done by returning her dowry* to her husband or asking permission from the courts, which could take at least three months. In Saudi Arabia, women are also culpable for sending 'nudes', and by nudes, I mean an image of their hair out. There is no consequence for the man receiving or asking for said text.

The rate at which men remarry is significantly high,

---

* An amount of property or money brought by a bride to her husband on their marriage.

and often soon after a divorce – within months in many cases. The story is not as simple for divorced women who from then on are considered damaged goods or baggage. A divorced woman is required to compromise and is considered 'lucky' if she should remarry. This was confirmed by the many examples I saw growing up of eligible women settling for ugly, fat and older men, or even men who were already married.

Love marriages are all about acting on feelings and having a loving, mutual connection before a ceremony takes place. You might think, given all I've written about arranged marriage here, that this sounds easier and yet, that is definitely not necessarily the case.

For the most part, I gained an understanding of Western marriages through watching romcoms like *Pretty Woman*. They showed me that, no matter how much the odds were stacked against her, a Western woman eventually landed on her feet to secure her Mr Right. There weren't any stigmas attached to her kissing a few frogs along the way, it was inevitable to get it wrong a few times. Where in my culture this was considered character destroying, in the Western world, it was character *building*. It felt like the Western woman had a monopoly on love, given I never saw an Asian protagonist in these roles.

The message in these love connections was that men would better women and increase their status, but these films only showed the noble and honourable men like Prince Charming. I did not see the pain or hurt that could be caused by men or love connections that didn't work. Without a balanced understanding, it was easy for me to be foolhardy about romance and succumb to the love symbology. Can we really say one form is better than the other? Each comes with its own struggles – and I sometimes think the stakes are even higher when there is love involved. Then men really do have the upper hand.

So, as you can imagine, if my understanding of the marriage and relationship part was lacking, my understanding of sex was non-existent.

I never had the birds and the bees conversation at home. This was partly my fault for avoiding the topic, though it felt like this disinterest was what was expected from me. I was led to believe only men wanted sex or even enjoyed sex. It was fine for them to be 'up for it'. It didn't add up to me because everyone either wanted it or was having it* and it was not just the guys. My schoolfriends were on dates and even making out in drama class. It was almost expected of

---

* I think I first realised how much I wanted sex listening to Toni Braxton's 'You're Makin' Me High'. Everything about the song oozes sexiness, despite the fact I didn't fully understand everything she was talking about back then.

us, anyone who didn't partake was shamed as 'frigid'. I even saw it within myself after I discovered soft porn when I was younger on Freeview, but I made sure to keep my interest in it hidden. I enjoyed it more for being my own pleasure and something that no one else had any say over or could interfere with.

Perhaps my deepest misunderstanding of sex was that a man would only have sex with me if he loved me. I didn't understand sex outside that context and equated sex with love. This might have been because I knew it usually happened between a married couple. I had no concept of whimsical, casual or opportunistic sex. The physical proximity that sex brought about implied to me an inevitable emotional proximity that I craved too. I didn't realise that emotional togetherness wasn't what was on men's minds during sex at all.

I saw sex and sexuality being celebrated by women of other races, but it felt like my sexuality as a Muslim woman was an inconvenience to the people around me. Whether it was men who couldn't understand my thirst or women reminding me to keep it classy and telling me to be less sexy in the name of female solidarity. It's been quite a juggling act being considered both a repressed hijabi* and yet too sexual.

Through using my voice and acting in a way I did not see Asian women behaving when I was growing up,

---

* A woman who wears a hijab, or scarf covering her head and neck.

I've achieved a lot of things that I wasn't taught were possible. But also by being commanding and analysing things that traditionally went unquestioned, it has at times felt like this has come at the cost of settling down in a relationship.

Despite this, I've always considered my sexuality to be a privilege and found the fun in it. I wanted to write my memoir as an honest account of a Muslim woman, a story I wish I had seen when I was growing up instead of books about Prince Charming, and women who were left to be saved.

In my life, there has been a lot to unpack in terms of tradition, but I was sceptical about the things that nobody talked about, such as premarital hook-ups and love, and I was willing to make my own decisions on these things. It feels well overdue that another account is shared rather than the same stories we've all heard before.*

It's time for the ugly sister to have her say.

---

* I'm also hoping the book will help me get a man.

Things I learnt from Bollywood* movies:

♡ Women are incapable of handling sexual advances and were passive in relationships.

♡ One man could take on a gang of five men with no weapons.

♡ Men only wanted innocent virgins or all unmarried women were virgins.

♡ A single woman was deemed to be a social reject and 'fair game'.

♡ Most people had a twin they didn't know about or were separated from.

♡ There was always a group of background dancers and musicians on standby – costume to boot.

♡ It was perfectly normal to break into song at any point in life.

♡ Helpfully, the lead actors are exceptional at singing and dancing, but no one ever referenced these skills outside of the musical sequences.

---

* Though some of the themes in Bollywood movies were valuable, it was not possible to capitalise on these to form a wider understanding without conversations in the house.

2

The First Wives Club

My mum was born in Kent, and she is very modern. She had been brought up on British and American TV shows like *Dynasty* and *The Persuaders*, she loved watching Joan Collins and she wasn't into Indian dramas, just the songs.

Though I've experienced people close to me having mental health issues throughout my life, mental health was never explained to me. My parent's generation felt a pressure to live up to an image of perfection, and for many women this became a self-imposed prison. Within this perfection, there was no room to be honest about your weaknesses, insecurities or doubts. It also meant some of these women grew to blame the people around them for the things that went wrong, because they found it impossible to conceive of any of the failings being their own. It led to some women becoming hardened and perpetuating the generational trauma and patterns of behaviour they'd experienced rather than finding a way to face or break them.

I didn't understand the importance of good mental health at all when I was growing up. My mum didn't appear to have friends and I didn't realise the potential negative impact of loneliness and isolation. Often it felt like she was just existing, rather than being independent and living. She threw herself into the routine of motherhood as a means of coping. Most of the time my mum managed so well and my father, and so the family generally, had a habit of downplaying and normalising it; for many Asians, it's seen as part and parcel of life. I often missed the signs of her illness when they were right there in front of me. Ultimately, my family's approach to anything unpleasant was not to talk about them. There could be multiple elephants in the room, but as long as we didn't address them, everything was fine. It didn't help that we had no extended family in the UK, so were different to most Asians who had plenty of relatives, and crucially social networks, to support them.

My mum was conscious of not letting her poor mental health impact on me. Often the person suffering either cannot bring themselves to ask for help or cannot fathom or communicate clearly what help they might need. At other times, it is all too easy to dismiss someone who does ask for help, because it is an invisible illness and difficult to see clearly what the problem is. One thing I have learnt through personal experience is that your mental health fluctuates, and that is why it's important to remember how things in the current moment are not how they will always be. It would have been good to have positive stories, growing up, that proved recovery was possible, rather than the narrative of it being lifelong.

My mum began struggling before I was born, shortly after her marriage to my dad. They had family in common and met in Delhi, when she was sixteen. Her father had sent her there from England, hoping family could teach her some of the values and discipline that he felt he couldn't instil. After staying at my father's family home for some time, my mum proposed to him. He was just a few years older than her, and my grand-father on my father's side gave my dad his blessing to pursue the marriage, believing my mum deserved love and a family. This made it both a love and a sort of arranged marriage, as they had vibes and so did their in-laws. They were not engaged for long before they got married in India.

My mother had to return to the UK though shortly afterwards. When she arrived back, she suffered a breakdown. This was likely for many reasons, but one of them was being separated from my father as he endured the lengthy immigration process to come to Britain from India. When my mum told me this story, it was the first example that I had that love, and men, could literally drive you crazy, and understandably I never wanted to go through that.

After a bumpy start, my mum and dad were reunited in the UK, and for a time they had a happy marriage. I didn't find it strange at the time, but growing up my mum and dad never kissed or even hugged in front of me. They loved watching the *Carry On* movies together and laughed at any sexual innuendo on television, so it wasn't that they were ashamed or ignorant of sex, it was just something they weren't accustomed to displaying openly. They wanted to be appropriate all the time, plus they hadn't seen their parents give any public displays of affection. Mum was happy but not fulfilled. Dad kept busy working and barely spent any time with mum. He liked keeping busy and his way of showing love, when he was home, was by tending to the housework.

This was the exact opposite of my experiences outside of home. Sex was everywhere. Literally. It was in conversations, it was in music, it was in the air. People were even doing it in alleyways. I would see women kerb-crawling on the way home from school. If they weren't doing it then they were probably trying to do it. I learnt that I had to play dumb at home and act like I knew everything around my friends. I remember not knowing what '69' was and no one telling me and feeling left out. It's not like anyone sent round a memo!

I thought of love and sex as the same thing and so didn't understand them as separate entities. There would be times where a woman's arousal would take centre stage in pop culture, albeit trivially, whether it was Sharon Stone in *Basic Instinct* or Demi Moore in *Ghost*, but even then, no one really talked about it, what it meant. It all felt taboo. I thought it was all going to come to a head when we had our first sex education class, only for that to turn out to be a cartoon. It was so disappointing! It was hosted by a silver robot with a cube-shaped head, much like in *Short Circuit*, flying in and out of bedrooms with a narrator talking about 'changes' and 'periods'. It was so bad that I already knew more than what the robot shared and my intelligence felt so insulted that I didn't ask any of the questions I had. We didn't even learn about contraception and I was off sick the day they tried to put a condom on a Bunsen burner!

At home, I didn't see any displays of healthy love but what I did see was obsession. My mum was completely besotted with my father. The more she tried to get closer to him, the more distance he would create. She was self-conscious of her illness and wanted to give him what she thought he wanted, she tried to be 'a good wife', but it wasn't clear to her what that was. He was money obsessed and that was something she couldn't give him. At times it felt like a love–hate relationship. He felt slighted that she was more British than him which he considered aspirational and something the man should possess more of.

Possibly mum was impacted by her own upbringing. As a young child, she had lost her mother to suicide and I found out later that my grandmother's depression could have been the result of domestic violence. We never spoke about it, largely because my mum wanted to protect my innocence.

All in all, my first templates for love, sex and marriage were confused and complicated at best. When your parents haven't had the best experience then you can't expect much for yourself and I assumed everything *bad* was normal. I had to muddle through – a girl with an Indian upbringing in a British world, with family problems in a society that expected perfection, and so I began my journey on unstable ground.

3

Clueless

I started wearing the hijab when I was nineteen years old, in 2006. It was a decision I made for myself with little thought as to what it would mean to others or how it would change the way I was perceived. Though I was changing my outer appearance, I was the same person.

I remember the first day wearing it and, due to it being a change, I was expecting questions from my friends and family, but no one so much as batted an eye. Wearing the hijab isn't a big ceremonial event in Islam, I simply chose to wear it one day. The media would have you believe otherwise, but it's more often than not down to the choice of the individual, especially in the West.

There wasn't a particular religious citation that drew my attention to the hijab. I had never spoken to anyone about its significance at home or at the madrassah.* There was literally zero education on the hijab† to form a balanced opinion about it. I had worn it to the madrassah as a young girl and I liked that it made me feel spiritually aware. Plus, I loved one of my teachers who taught there, and she wore it. I wanted to be just like her and so she inspired me in a way. I wondered as a child why I didn't wear my hijab outside of Saturday school, and for the most part I think it was due to fear. I felt cowardly for avoiding the hijab in my teens, it felt bold and yet refined, and it was so uncommon back then. It was my fear of change I was trying to resist by choosing to embrace the hijab. In the Muslim-friendly environment I was in, I wasn't treated any differently wearing it, and was my own person. The hijab/burka‡ wasn't reductive. I had no idea of quite how different that would be outside of the bubble I was in.

In my teens, I would say I was a conscientious Muslim. I recited prayers, fasted and I tried to be a just person. My mother said she'd dabbled in the hijab for a short period of time in her teens before removing it. So, there wasn't any pressure from home to wear

---

* Islamic Saturday school.

† A head-covering worn in public by some Muslim women.

‡ A long, loose garment covering the whole body from head to feet.

it. In fact, my parents liked me dressing in English or 'modern' clothes as they liked to call them.

I wonder if an element of me dressing traditionally was a way of rebelling against my parents, at least subconsciously. My parents, the immigrant generation, wanted so badly to assimilate,* at any cost, leaving me with the legacy of their compromise. It meant that I had to settle rather than explore the different facets of my culture. I was neither allowed to be too Indian nor too British, and so I couldn't fully appreciate either. It was a life full of boundaries, and the reminders of boundaries, without a break.

Much like a bride, my existence as an Asian growing up in England seemed to be to impress others or to conform, rather than to let loose and embrace my culture and identity in the way I wanted, without judgement. Given there were so many things that were not permissible in my culture (tattoos, drinking, fillers), wearing the hijab was one of the few 'halal' ways of being a rebel. I didn't need anyone's approval, nor did I have to ask for my parent's permission, I wore it because I wanted to.

The hijab gave me a sense of pride in my appearance and a way of tailoring my look. It added style to my

---

* Assimilate means to adjust or conform to greater society in order to fit in. There isn't ever an expectation for white people to assimilate.

outfits, and I relished going shopping in Green Street to pick up a new one whenever I could. I started by securing it triangularly, as that was the easiest way and you only needed one safety pin. As my confidence grew, I wrapped longer rectangular scarves which were more common at the time. You could wrap it any way you wanted, I learnt, and the variation was exciting. I was always on the lookout for a new hijab. I really liked the bright ones, and I had an ever-growing collection in different colours and fabrics.

Despite my love for the hijab and the style, I know I approached the decision to wear it naïvely. Given I had only felt acceptance from those around me, it led me to expect this from everyone. I didn't think something as small as wearing a hijab would change anything. However, in a short space of time, the scarf completely transformed the way in which people would interact with me. It sent a message to others that I neither intended, nor could I control. Muslims were proud at the sight of me wearing one and would endow me with qualities simply because I was wearing it like a 'kumari'* or 'habiba', meaning 'good girl'.

I remember an Asian man who saw me wearing it for the first time commented that, 'I looked better'. I had mixed feelings about this. I knew his heart was in the right place, but talk about a backhanded compliment.

---

* Prepubescent, unplucked girl.

I mean, my hair was great before! I think what he meant was that the image I was projecting was better, more in line with his standards. Either way he was only thinking about the way I looked and not who I was. I wasn't wearing the hijab for this attention, nor because I was an angel. It put me on a pedestal where I did not belong and left me helpless to do anything but try and balance there. This idolisation of me in a hijab was problematic, not least because many people who didn't wear hijab were better practising Muslims than me. Though I wasn't a fraud, it was hard not to feel like one given these reactions.

Hilariously, I was a better practising Muslim when I didn't wear a headscarf, although I didn't realise that until later. The reason I kept wearing it, despite its challenges, was twofold: I didn't want to go back on the decision I had made (I'm stubborn like that) and I didn't want to believe that people were so stupid as to think that if someone looked different they were lesser.

What the hijab removed, unbeknown to me, was my personal identity. I had no space to develop my own self. The hijab slowly morphed into my identity until I couldn't differentiate between me and the headscarf. Who I was and what I could be was all sidelined as my unofficial and unpaid day job as the Islamic trivia communicator and translator took precedence. Non-Muslim co-workers and passers-by stopped speaking to me and started speaking at me.

'Can your husband see your hair?'
'Are you allowed anal before marriage?'
'Which way do you have to face during sex?'
'Do you have to do everything a man wants in
   bed, as you have to obey the man in Islam?'
'What does Islam say about women's rights?'
'Why don't men have to cover their hair?'
'Why do men cover their hair?' (Wrong religion
   entirely.)
'Are you allowed to drink water during your fast?'
'Why aren't you allowed to eat pork?'
'Have you ever tried bacon?'
'You ain't allowed a drink? Corr, I couldn't do
   that!'

Before wearing the hijab, my ethnicity and faith wasn't immediately obvious as I was fair skinned and I could often 'pass' for different cultures. Once I made the decision to wear it, I was no longer just me, I was representing all Muslims, and that was something I never signed up for. Now on top of living up to the expectations of my community, I was also expected to please a wider community who had little or poor knowledge of Islam. Usually at my own detriment. If I even so much as held a guy's hand in public, people would judge me despite not knowing anything about my religion. I had to double-check, and sometimes triple-think, everything for everyone else, with no thanks.

Worst of all was that the headscarf made my pain invisible. People were oblivious or unsympathetic to my plight. I was both hyper-visible and invisible to those around me. They wanted things from me but they didn't want to know *me*. If that isn't messy, I don't know what is.

One thing I learnt was that the narrative of the hijab was closely linked to its role in preserving a woman's piety, particularly a married woman. And so, I wasn't prepared how I would be perceived as a single hijabi. The two things just didn't go together.* Questions about my unknown-to-me betrothed followed me around.

'*Marshallah*,'† they would say, 'are you getting married?'

And, 'Congratulations, when is your marriage?'

Lo and behold I was betrothed to the hijab.

I was single but wearing the unofficial uniform of a married woman.‡ Sisters in Christianity could opt out of getting married, but that wasn't the case in Islam. Marriage was one half of my faith.§ So even though I was wearing a hijab, which protected me from the

---

* It was hard to both be pious and of interest to men.

† Praise be to God.

‡ It was the same reaction when I got my nose pierced. It got flicked off during a facial!

§ Marriage is highly recommended though not obligatory in Islam (Dr Bilal Philips).

male gaze, I wasn't complete without a husband. Men always had to be in my business in some shape or form.

At the beginning, it didn't affect me because I had no intention of getting married. I wanted to find love and not marriage and most of us know those are two different things.* If I could have both then great, but everything I saw felt like it was a compromise of one over the other. It turned out, in the hijab, I wasn't able to find either. It made it hard for people to separate me from the object. They presumed they knew me and what was good for me/what I wanted, without caring to.

The hijab communicated my marital status for me. It was so loud that I couldn't compete with it or tame it. I mean, I can't lie, part of wanting to be seen as 'good' and putting on the hijab was undeniably because I wanted to catch a certain type of man. But this seemed an impossible feat given the right man didn't come with a similar symbol attached. The word 'RIGHT MAN' plastered across his forehead would have been nice. Instead, I would have to look beyond a man's appearance as he would mine. Sadly, the hijab just made guys I was interested in trivialise me and sometimes pick on me as it muted my gender/sexuality.

---

* For some Asian men I had to be married to earn rights. If I dated outside of marriage, I was regarded as a harlot and 'fair game' and therefore beneath compassion.

I remember, as a teenager, an Asian college kid using the word 'aunty' to denigrate me. It wasn't the look any guy was going to go for and I got the impression from some guys that all they were fascinated with was my headscarf's removal (like panties). If the hijab was something a guy was into then that wasn't someone who I really wanted to get to know: it's very creepy to be fetishised like that. My sexuality was nothing to do with covering my hair, and the way some of these guys linked the hijab to sex was gross.

Not only in sex was my hijab co-opted and vilified, but it also became politicised. Unbeknown to me, it gave off political intent, despite the fact that I am apolitical. The hijab didn't look British and apparently that made it unacceptable and so I had to work harder to earn or maintain my British status than others because of it, and that didn't mean eating more bland food. To me, Britain is simply the place where I was born and doesn't bear any deeper meaning beyond that. I tried not to let it bother me because even if I removed the veil, I still wouldn't appear British enough, at the end of the day I would still be Brown.

I was completely naïve to the possibility that it might be a symbol that was alienating. When I first put on the hijab it was post 9/11 There wasn't any way the average Muslim on the street could have foreseen the war on terror, much less a young Muslim like me, who didn't go out much. After 9/11, the hijab became more widely adopted by domestic Muslims, partly given the increase in people discovering Islam for themselves. It was arguably the only thing of its time to grow in popularity and notoriety in parallel.

As the fear of terrorism grew, my relationship with the hijab changed again. From being a once-treasured accessory, it became a red flag for the general public to cross the street from me, to raise their guard around me and to distance themselves from me. This was compounded by the fact that, despite doing this, no one wanted to share how they felt or have the difficult conversations that might result from that. Most of the time they didn't want to be openly disparaging, partly out of political correctness. The conversations I used to have with white people no longer held an underlying need to exhibit tolerance for me, and there were far fewer exchanges than before. Either they looked at the ground, or if they were feeling brave they tried to force a smile in order to say, 'I know it's not you, but could you try and have a word with your people?'

It became a struggle and a conscious effort, at times, to keep it on my head given the negative connotations the hijab became associated with, compared with when I didn't really have to give it any thought when I had started wearing it. There was now an increased risk attached to wearing it, that if I was extremely unlucky, I could fall victim to a hate crime. This hatred and mistrust only fuelled the vicious cycle of Muslims feeling withdrawn, which reinforced society's belief that Muslims were outsiders and didn't try enough to assimilate. The hijab couldn't stop me from assimilating with British culture however, I wasn't prepared to have to fight my own battles as a Brown woman, as well as those of the hijab.

When the debate about wearing religious symbols and the hijab, particularly in public spaces, became increasingly discussed, it was hard to take in. Overnight, the hijab had gone from being no one's business to everyone's. I would hear reports on the news that I was oppressed. I wondered what they knew about my life that I didn't. If this was such a common belief, then why had no one so much as asked whether I was OK or if I needed help? People treated the hijab like a do not disturb sign and they felt like this let them off the hook. It felt like an impossible situation because if I removed the veil then surely the anti-Muslims and terrorists won, the anti-Muslims by my change in dress and the terrorists by making me feel like an outsider in the country they were aggrieved to see me settled in.

The hijab, which was just a garment to express modesty, had been co-opted.

When I was twenty-four, despite the fact I had worn it for five years, I suddenly found myself in the position of having colleagues and even strangers who wanted me to explain the hijab and why I wore it. I've had friends and strangers alike tell me to 'just take it off'. One told me within five minutes of meeting me I would never find a man wearing a headscarf as it 'looked strange' and detracted from my beauty. There was possibly a certain truth to that, but it's tough having to listen to a non-Muslim man tell me how he thinks I should dress as a Muslim woman in a non-Muslim country, in order for me to have a better quality of life. It was attitudes to the hijab rather than it itself that made wearing it so challenging.

These critics of Islamic attire claimed to have the best interests of women at heart. They didn't seem to have an issue with Muslim men's attire. Just women's, and it was for our own good. There was never any consideration from the requestor as to the personal implications of breaking from a long-term obligation to oneself. It was simply suggested that if I removed the hijab then it would make things a whole lot easier. But for whom? Me or society?

Why did I have to change? The scarf was a bigger deal to others than it ever was to me. I couldn't understand the fascination with a head-covering. The constant correction of people's misguided beliefs that I was oppressed left me in a state of denial about the times when I actually was. Not by my faith or attire, but by situations in life, and therefore I was isolated to cope with these alone. Also if I showed any sign of struggling or raised an issue, I would just be confirming people's incorrect assumptions about the hijab, that it was a cause for concern, so I was forced to repress my feelings and hold them in.

Frustratingly, I didn't see non-Muslim celebrities who chose to wear the hijab – like say Rihanna, who wore it for elaborate magazine photoshoots in Muslim countries like Dubai, or Angelina Jolie, the sweetheart of the UN – face the stigma Muslim women were facing for doing the exact same thing. These women were not considered oppressed and subservient – quite the contrary, they were seen as being culturally sensitive. It was even liberating and ethical of them.

It seemed the hijab was only appropriate when it was being appropriated.

When it came to the hijab, white people were focused on how it affected and made non-Muslims uncomfortable – missing the point in that it simply wasn't about them. Right or wrong, the decision should have been mine to make and to live with rather than, as with everything else, to be concerned with how it impacted others. So many Western cultural decisions didn't affect us so why couldn't it work the other way around? I didn't start causing a fuss when it came to Ascot season, fox-hunting or Crufts.*

To satisfy others, it felt like I was being forced to

---

* An international annual dog show in the UK.

choose sides between religion or society, when I had affiliations with and related to both. Without being able to fully show allegiance to either one, the scarf made some fringes of society distrustful towards me as they couldn't understand why I would choose to look different if I felt part of the same society as them. And while I still wear the scarf, it's something I choose to do for me, no one else. It isn't some profound deference on my part nor a battle, it's something that matters to me.

The hijab has taught me a great deal. It's made me more sensitive to the way we should accept people, even if they happen to be under-represented or mis-represented by/to the majority. It has shown me that I shouldn't judge a book by its cover and helped me appreciate that people are so special, and that unique-ness should be celebrated. It has reinforced for me that we can and should be supportive to people that main-stream society shuns for not living up to its ridiculous and unattainable ideals. As someone who character-istically doesn't fit in, it's helped me see people for who they really are, rather than just the social cues that they emit.*

As others had not grown in the same way as me, the visible religious attire left me wide open to scrutiny that was inescapable. This was from both within Muslim

---

* At the cost of dick. It is a massive contraceptive and guys literally cross the road and turn corners to avoid it.

circles and outside. Muslims judged me for being too liberal and non-Muslims judged me for being too conservative and oppressed. There was neither compassion nor understanding from either camp. It was frustrating that the hijab meant people who didn't even know me took me for granted. Maybe if they took the time to do so, they'd realise I'm caring, funny, sweet, chatty, and so much more. Their loss.

How to tell when a hijabi is having a bad hair day:

1. She's smiling.
2. She has a spring in her step.
3. She's singing.
4. She's busting a move.
5. The drinks are on us.

Because no one can see we are having a bad hair day . . .

4

Eat, Pray, No Love

Western bases	Muslim bases
1st base: Kissing	1st base: Eye contact
2nd base: Fingering	2nd base: Smiling
3rd base: Oral stimulation	3rd base: Exchanging numbers
4th base: Sex	4th base: Seeing woman's hair*

When I was nineteen, I had no social life and all I did was work at Asda. A few months into getting the role, I started wearing hijab, but it changed nothing as I was never going to be a social butterfly no matter how colourful or fun my headscarves were.

That's when I first discovered men in real life, beyond

---

* In Islam I can be in 1st-3rd bases at the same time!

Bollywood. I never had to consort with 'the other side', i.e. boys, until then. There was a feeling that this was the same for the other Asian boys and girls who worked there too. It felt exciting, but also risky given there was no protocol, and we were free of the watchful eyes of a teacher or wali. There was one fit guy that all the girls liked. He was a 'bad boy' Asian with slick, black hair. He worked on the rotisserie counter and once I walked by and he said out loud, as though I was also a piece of meat from his counter, within earshot, 'I ain't trying to get married.' I glanced in his direction and realised he was talking to me. So that's how men in general saw me. I was 'wifey' material and most guys like him were not looking for a wife at all.

I thought his apprehension was because I was sweet, chubby, as opposed to the model type. The guys I liked didn't tend to notice me. I had huge breasts, which sadly didn't help my cause. That feels a travesty of injustice as my breasts were neither here nor there, as far as guys viewed me. I was the 'good girl', 'a sister' and 'reliable', given all my exchanges with men were platonic and respectful. The problem was the guys I was really into weren't my equivalent – the 'good boy', 'brother' or 'reliable' type. I had crushes on colleagues, but those men laughed them off, if they even noticed in the first place.

Since Asian men didn't see me as a romantic option, many of them treated me as one of the guys. Kashif, a friend, told me, 'Some men want to marry a pure woman but have their fun on the side. They want to maintain their wife's piety.' It was sad to consider that when a woman becomes a wife these men believe she couldn't possibly be as 'naughty' or 'sexual' as the women they have flings with. In fact, this goes against Islamic teachings where it is a man's duty to fulfil his partner's needs. There's a hadith* that says, 'Do not engage in sexual intercourse with your wife like hens; rather, firstly engage in foreplay with your wife and flirt with her and then make love to her.' (You can tell a lot about a man from the way he gives head – in many ways, all you need to know.)

It made me exasperated to think that as an Asian woman all I could hope for was a marriage where the man cheats. That even if I found someone, *I* was expected to live up to some out-dated version of a saint because he probably wanted to sleep around. It only confirmed that I had taken the correct stance in avoiding marriage.

It was an age where knowledge alone made me culpable – when it was incumbent on me to be pure. No one alluded to what the consequences would be if I went over to the 'bad side'; it was just understood that it wasn't respectable. There was a feeling or threat that

* Alliyatul Muttaqin, p. 110.

marriage would be the way to tame me* – if I were lucky enough to find someone who'd have me.

The community considered me affiliated if I played my part and followed the rules. The price to belong within this coveted community felt high, and the conditions attached were not ones that I felt that Black or white communities placed on one another. I abstained from boyfriends, didn't wear make-up and dressed appropriately, but the community didn't know me in any real sense so I didn't know if I could go by their judgement to decide if I was good. From the smiles of strangers, I inferred that they considered me good by default, unless I proved otherwise, and so the fear of being outcast lingered with me. I got the impression that showing willing was all that mattered to my so-called community. This left people who took a different route to figure it out by themselves. This was because they were disregarded and weren't spoken to, rather spoken about in the past tense: 'Don't even mention her name, she's gone off the rails.'

This expectation to be good, without having seen the world, felt unforgiving. Good to me was meaning it rather than acting it out performatively. I wanted to be good but there wasn't any threshold for bad or

---

* Marriage was often viewed as a means to treat a long list of ailments and, in certain cases, superseded medicine.

mistakes, especially if it was wrong to talk about them. My understanding of sex was that abstinence could be bartered for acceptance in the community, and that didn't feel good at all. If they knew the truth, that it wasn't that I didn't have the inclination, rather it was circumstantial, that I wasn't getting laid, I don't think they'd be so accepting of me. I wanted to give my flower away, but no one wanted it. I was shy around the guys I liked, plus I looked too sweet for them to take me seriously. I think my hijab-wearing good deeds had diminishing returns because, fine, I wasn't freemixing*, but it wasn't due to possessing insurmountable willpower, it was because the boys didn't want me. I didn't learn willpower because of this and so was crippled by temptation each and every time it arose.

I couldn't relate to the shame that was attached to sex. It was just one aspect of a relationship. If anything, the taboo only made it more enigmatic, and to some of these guys more enticing. I didn't know or understand what the obsession with piety hoped to achieve. Was there a Muslim husband's club where they competed in a 'my wife is purer than yours' Olympics? The only way that piety could be considered a workable concept would be if it applied to men too, which was laughable and in direct conflict with their biology. If a man was

---

* The interaction between genders.

pure, it was a worry, and his family would wonder if everything was all right with him.

It's dangerous when women are viewed as pure or impure. I'm vast and complex and I couldn't comprehend what was to be gained from such banal and singular definitions. If as a woman I was pure, the idea of dick 'tainting' me ranged from a strange fetish to the unhealthy mindset of sex being a dirty forbidden act, as opposed to a healthy human need. It was both problematic and not conducive to a happy and fulfilling sex life. Conversely, if as a woman I was impure, what did that imply? I shouldn't have to forfeit being treated respectfully because I didn't conform to narrow and outdated ideals. Women shouldn't be judged based on arbitrary levels of piety.

Could I be honourable all the time? If so, to what end? I wondered if there was such a thing as 'wasted honour'. Imagine honourable women that were unrecognised, unmarried and too *honourable* to do anything with. That seemed pointless to me. If a person wanted to be pure it should be for themselves, not anybody else. Because I believed men were indifferent, guys didn't want pure; they'd just been taught to think they did. As Kashif had said to me, 'Men would sleep with anything.' That proved their standards weren't exactly stratospheric, so why were we trying to sustain something impractical and, ultimately, unrealistic?

In a world where there's next to no sex education

for Asian women and no outlet for us to learn about sexuality, let alone express it, we should treat each other with empathy as we are all learning and growing. I may not always get it right but gone are the days where I am as good as community property. I think the reasons I wasn't sanctimonious about it is because, as I wasn't having sex, I knew it wasn't all I had and that I had more to offer.

I was bigger than my vagina, and that's bigger than you think!

5

Late Graduation

I lost my friendship with Kashif when he was arranged to be married. He'd flown back to Pakistan to marry the woman his mother had lined up for him. We never said goodbye, but once his mother had sent him a picture of the bride and he'd said yes, it felt like we were on different life paths. He did infer that I should find someone, but I couldn't begin to fathom it. I couldn't marry a stranger, and that's all men were to me.

I realise now I'm older that friendships come and go like this, and for me, being a bit of a nomad, this happened often. Friends are there for reasons, seasons or for life, but when so many of my Asian friends would be married off each season – for a number of reasons – the life friendships just didn't last. I was always OK with it. Besides, there's a lot to be said about living in your own little world.

I think my work at Asda and trying to make my way (or even just exist) in life had distracted me because, like an idiot, I had forgotten how to recite the Quran.* As a young child, aged six, I learnt it very quickly and hadn't revisited it since I'd completed recitation classes. Again, a reluctance to be considered as 'traditional' played a part in this. I hadn't read it in so long that when I was twenty years old and tried to read it, I found I had completely forgotten Arabic.

My local mosque gave lessons and I joined them. The only catch was that the students were all ten to fourteen years old, so I was the uncool older kid in class. The classes were different from those I went to as a child. In addition to Arabic, the teacher was also quite determined to teach us discipline. She was a stern, older woman, known for her short temper and yelling, sometimes even smacking disobedient children. She also had a reputation for throwing kids out of class who were caught talking.

Fortunately, I wasn't the only older student. I was joined by a revert† named Khadija, a young Black woman who was also the teacher's assistant. I had

---

* Holy book in Islam.

† In Islam we believe everyone begins life as a Muslim. A revert is therefore someone who comes back to the Islamic faith.

been attending classes for months and picked up the language again slowly but surely. In one class after I'd finished reading in front of the teacher, the teacher pulled me to one side and said, 'I want to talk to you.' I instantly knew it wasn't going to be good. From experience, it was never good when someone announced they wanted to talk to me – otherwise they would simply just say what it was. It was like someone saying, 'I've got a bone to pick with you'. That could wake you up quicker than a shot of coffee and fill your stomach with the same dread of the shits.

The class ended and as the kids clambered out of the circle we had formed on the floor, and went to put their shoes on, I stayed back. The teacher kept a poker face and asked me directly, 'Are you looking for someone?'

'I'm not sure,' I replied coyly.

I was conscious of the punishment that might befall me for not playing ball. It was hardwired into me that my default response to men should always be no unless it was marriage. It was very strange being expected to deny the very thing that, for most people, underpinned my existence.

'I know someone, he's a cousin of mine. He's trying to come into the country soon,' she said uncertainly.

It was a shock. I had never seen her like this, she was usually so dominating and so sure.

Alarm bells started going off in my head – they needed a woman who was a British citizen to help get him into the country. I had saved myself for far too long to sacrifice myself in order to rescue some random guy.

'No, thank you, I'm not looking right now. I'm still young.' I smiled knowing that I wasn't young to her. I was the student too old for this class. It was to throw her off the scent and imply that I had more living left to do when in actual fact I had no game plan and didn't know whether I was coming or going.

She wilfully ignored my response. 'I can show you a photo if you want. Let me know.'

'OK,' I responded uncomfortably. I left the room, put on my shoes and made my way down the stairs and towards home.

It blew my mind that there I was in the house of God, in worship, being propositioned like this. Not even directly by the gentleman, I might add.* At least I could have been left with an 'I've still got it' vibe if he'd asked me directly, but instead what I had was a British passport which vetoed my pussy – it wasn't a good feeling. This was just how it could happen. Someone asked a young woman for her hand in marriage on behalf of a man she'd never met and if she said yes, then all of a sudden she was married to a stranger and her whole life was changed for ever.

I wondered if this was what making friendships in my community would mean? Being pushed towards

---

* Mosques have separate areas for males and females.

random men I had never met nor wanted to meet. Was this also what Kashif had in mind for me? It wasn't an attractive option and it made me want to hide away more than ever before. I could be minding my own business and the next minute I'm being offered up as a snack for men who may not even brush their teeth after eating paan.* It made my stomach turn.

I prayed the teacher would forget, and she never brought it up again. Maybe she asked Khadija next, though I hope not.

---

* Paan is a preparation combining betel leaf with areca nut widely consumed throughout Southeast Asia, and East Asia.

6

The One

Pretty boy, or the brag artist

Classically known for running through a list of all the women he's been with (of which there are loads) to your face like an accomplishment. Doesn't remember your name, no attention to detail and probably carries around a mirror or checks himself out in his iPhone camera every hour. Will cheat, probably in front of you.

The doctor

Aside from his duty of care, the lure of a doctor* for me would be his salary and spending his money while he's working eighteen-hour shifts. Also, when he doesn't return my calls I can't be mad as he's probably saving someone's life. Downside is he could be cheating with another doctor – or maybe I've watched too much *Grey's Anatomy*? Either way, their life partners are preordained for them before or during their conception.

Nice guy

He will do anything for you but is too clingy and will eventually give you the ick.

Mummy's boy

Will put his mum/family before anyone else. Could work if you're into the Oedipus-complex vibe.

---

* A doctor could always double up as a Deliveroo driver and fetch me things, but I wouldn't have a Deliveroo driver sub as a doctor. (Unless he was studying medicine and just doing Deliveroo driving to make ends meet. Ladies, I think that might just be the perfect man).

Deliveroo driver

This is a roadman and spends a minimum of eighteen hours on the streets hustling between different food delivery services. He delivers for the home but not the heart. He puts his brothers or 'the homies' before anyone else. No woman could compete with his penchant for bromance.

Tortured soul

Musicians, comedians, writers and so on. He will understand you and that will be attractive, but they are a little damaged and so these characters certainly require compromise. They can be emotionally selective and unavailable until they decide what it is they want. It's unlikely most of them ever will.

Waste

The guy who gets women to pay for everything and runs up a 'promise to pay you back' tab.

Listener

He is undeniable and great sex. It's like he knows you better than you know yourself. The prospects with the listener will depend on what he does immediately after sex and whether that's looking at his phone, an encore or a hug.

The One

At the risk of being hated, the concept of 'The One' could stop you from pursuing 'the current one' who could become 'The One'. Don't let the fear of your feelings or an image of your ideal future boyfriend/husband make you miss what's staring you in the face.

Note: on rare occasions there may be overlap between two to three of the above.

In my late teens, it felt like a rite of passage to fall in love. Everyone around my age was waiting for it to happen. My girlfriends would deliberate over whether they were in love or not and who might be falling for them.

I was aggrieved to accept the noise around me about love. That love was everything and that men could drive you crazy. Watching my dad's impact on my mum, I felt it my duty to learn from it and break the cycle.

I remember not getting it. For a long time. I couldn't understand why everyone would act all foolish when it came to the 'L' word.* My mum sometimes let loose and would break into song: 'I'm feeling quite insane and young again / And all because I'm mad about the boy.'† How could something be so all-encompassing?

I was strait-laced, rational and level-headed, so it would take a lot more to get me to lose my head. It seemed ridiculous and so counter-intuitive that I should allow myself to potentially be hurt. I was sceptical about it, though I was drawn to the symbolism. I doubted it would happen for me.

Love was everywhere but I didn't know what it meant. There were millions of love songs and movies dedicated to it. Although I could see how it made people feel, there was no explanation of what love really meant. I would talk to friends, teachers, colleagues about it and they'd look at me and give me cryptic messages.

'It's the best feeling in the world.'

'Don't ever fall in love, it will ruin your life!'

'Love makes it all worth it.'

'You just have to feel it and then you'll understand.'

'Your time will come.'

---

* At times it felt that she was more infatuated with the idea of love itself, rather than the way it manifested.

† From 'Mad About The Boy', lyrics by Noel Coward.

The One

No one could ever tell me what it was, I had to figure it out for myself, like the matrix.

I was mystified by the odds and thought it would be incredibly lucky if I bumped into the right person where I lived in Leyton. Was this the postcode I could entrust my heart to?

It seemed as though 'The One' was not actually promised to anyone and that there would be a lot of frogs along the way, and as an Asian, I was loath to get it wrong.

7

Fair Deal

I actively avoided Bollywood movies and Indian dramas to steer clear of the relationship politics they high-lighted, but often I felt like a 'bad Asian' for not soaking up more Asian culture. I understood Hindi but spoke my mother tongue poorly, often mixing both Urdu and English words in the same sentence. My parents preferred me to speak English and I gravitated towards British culture which I took for my primary culture. I also thought the more British I was, the less guys would want to marry me and the more they'd want to date me. At the same time as supporting me assimilating into British culture, my parents would remind me I wasn't English, and non-familial uncles would tell me repeatedly, 'Don't forget where you're from!' They were reminding me not to forget who I really am or my heritage. The feelings that swelled inside of me living in this cultural paradox would haunt me for years to come. My parents wanted me to hold fast to something they themselves hadn't taught me – my Indian roots. They would both reward my British behaviour and chastise me when I was acting 'too English' and so it was never clear where the line was.

In relationships, this cultural paradox became even more clear. Asian guys had defined expectations of what a woman should be, but these were not always well-articulated. As I was Asian, I was expected to automatically know what the term 'traditional' meant, but that is subjective. To some this could mean dress, to others your attitude or accent – often it is simply summarised as one's 'mindset'. Clearly all the differences in opinion of what 'traditional' Indian connections meant left plenty of space for misunder-standing, and with the pressure of trying to make a connection quickly, ran the risk of setting couples up for a fall.

Like the stand-ups I loved watching on TV, Bill Hicks, Chris Rock and Patrice O'Neal, I had a big mouth. There is an expectation that an Indian bride is passive and obedient – and that isn't me at all. I'm from the *ghetto*, and tell it how it is. I would not conform, not even for dick. It was this reluctance to play the game and show willing that held me back. If I could only show that I could be what a man wanted, then I might possibly have settled down. But even the term 'settled' doesn't feel worth the sacrifices necessary. I want a man to want me for me, not the person I could impersonate most of the time. If I have to give up everything, then I want the world.

Besides, even without my additional demands, the odds are not good. I fancied Asian men, but it's no secret there are fewer Asian men to Asian women, so they are in huge demand. Unfortunately, they also know this and it makes them cocky and arrogant. A lot of them think they can have anyone they want because they have been raised as though pussy is their birthright.

I also had my suspicions that the official story wasn't the full story. Occasionally I'd hear of a friend of a friend having a love marriage. In these instances, they had married despite their parents not giving their full blessing. These love marriages proved that there was more to marriage than being a Stepford Wife. I felt a little vindicated by that, even though it was still a mystery to me what the secret to the love part was.

I'd hear from newlyweds how a lot of men weren't that concerned with culinary delights. Some men didn't even like chapatis!* They didn't want the bedroom to be impacted by what was going on in the kitchen and

---

* Indian flatbreads.

saw it as a trade-off – that the more of a homemaker someone was, the further it lowered their kudos as a sexual deity. This made sense to me as it felt like behaving honourably required you to be treated with the same honour in return. If I didn't make so much of an effort to be the perfect homemaker, then I'd stand a better chance of getting my back blown out in the bedroom. Guys didn't really want to be fucking up – like 'what a great catch, she's so pure and so honourable and so skilled at making chapatis'. Guys wanted to fuck down in a 'you can't cook, dirty bitch' type of deal. Sex is always better with a bit of healthy animosity.*

So men want to sleep with a whore, just not marry one. What a conundrum! If I wasn't a whore, he wouldn't want to sleep with me, and if I was one, he wouldn't want to marry me. That was the game. I had to be both and know which one to be when.

From the couples around me, the most successful relationships I saw were instances where a strong woman trapped a man and made it seem like it was his idea. To date, I think this is the best strategy. My more traditional acquaintances opted to have their matters arranged formally by attending 'Muslim matrimonial events', sort of like *Love Island* but where contestants are fully dressed and instead of a sum of money at the end, the prize up

---

* There's a difference between making love and fucking – this is specifically about the latter.

for grabs is a wedding. These MMEs are held in auditoriums around the country, where the mixing of genders is treated as though it is rare, and so highly vetted by the event organisers. They remind me of finishing school, a place where, as a woman, my participation would have to be a balance between knowing where to look at all times and an eagerness to find a life partner. It felt so orchestrated that it didn't feel like a place I could be my usual self or show any interest in the guy.

That's if I was even lucky enough to get near one.

On paper, the numbers were shocking with at least twenty Muslim women to every Muslim man. It made me wonder, if the odds are so far stacked in the man's favour, how far would a woman have to compromise? This felt like the wrong strategy for a fair deal. I also felt put off by the fact that as these events are ticketed, people would be profiting from people trying to find The One. I'm sure that people who are willing to pay more would be given a priority, which basically left the event for everyone else a place for same-sex singletons to mingle among each other and maybe exchange a few tips.

The only criteria I know for sure is I want him to be Muslim, whether that's before he meets me or after converting – either way is fine. I don't want to date someone who I have to explain everything to, but like with the hijab, society would presume that I am under the rule of a man rather than it being a partnership. I underestimated the joys a man could bring, resigning myself to the way I felt men saw women – as a piece of meat.

I am very sceptical about true love as I've never seen it for myself in real life. If I date a Muslim man it would be great, but where would I find him? More to the point, how could I even give him the green light? All of it seems so complicated and the important stuff like love and companionship is so downplayed or misconstrued as hoochie-licious it hardly seems worth the hassle.

As time went on, I realised I so badly wanted to be chosen by the right mystery man, who is still to make himself known, that I hadn't even considered the qualities that would make him the right partner for me. It was all about how I would have to manipulate my qualities and identity to fit him.

From my culture to the way I speak, from my cooking skills to being able to throw it down in the bedroom, my focus was on the wrong things. I didn't need to change, I needed someone to add to me and lift me up. Unfortunately, in my early twenties I didn't appreciate this and, without any solid footing or guidance, was leaving myself wide open to getting it wrong with a lot of frogs (including most of the types of men I listed earlier) in order to fully understand the value in what I brought to the table.

These sex bombs would provide me with some excellent stories (great for comedy!), but some very damaged self-worth (also great for comedy!).

8

Supernova

I couldn't keep up with recitation classes as I had found a job at a call centre in the city. The role involved long hours and shift work and so I'd never make it back in time for classes. I was fluent enough to continue finishing the Quran myself at least, and I was glad to avoid further proposals of marriage from strangers. Even at twenty-two, I was a reliable worker, but I had a distinct lack of direction and had no idea where my life was headed. I moved from an insurance call centre to a call centre for a posh bank that had celebrity clients such as landowners, musicians, footballers, the lot.

I had always loved writing, but I had no idea how to get into journalism or publishing. I had writing samples and I knew my ideas were good, but it just felt like it was impossible. I applied for a role with an Asian magazine.

Surely I had the edge as an Asian and it would guarantee me a spot?

Wrong!

I was told by the magazine that they were looking for more diversity and so they hired a girl named Leanne from Chelsea.

Following this, I applied to a well-known white woman's magazine (fronted by a comedian) and was told that they didn't have space for my voluntary, unpaid work as they were on the brink of collapse (they're still around today). I now know this was code for 'I wasn't in with the in-crowd enough to be entertained'. I'm not privileged enough to even confront the male gatekeepers, that was the boss level. Instead, I was still on level one – facing the female gatekeepers. I even reached out to a magazine well known for covering diaspora experiences but I don't think I was the right ethnic vibe as I never got a reply to my initial or follow-up emails. For an industry that shouts about change and diversifying their content, they didn't like to put their money where their mouth is.

Diversity had become industrialised and therefore bigger than the people it was supposedly uplifting. The reason it could be so hard for me being a person of colour within this dynamic is that there is always a pressure to be more than I am, to perform, even though in most cases it is just to tick a box. It is a Catch-22 situation, I can't get the work unless I have experience and I can't get the experience without the work. I suppose it didn't help that I had zero style and people would snigger at me but were usually too thoughtful to tell me how they really felt. The narrative to support BAMEs* was gaining such momentum that the impression was as though I could get by on my ethnicity and my ethnicity alone. But in my case, no one was willing to give me that first opportunity.

My manager at the bank call centre was a man named Steve, and he was cool. He was tall, ginger and wore glasses; he was good vibes even if he did use the phrase 'cool beans'. It was at my first monthly appraisal since I'd been working there, a much-welcomed hour off the phones, and Steve asked me what I wanted to be. I had always wanted to be a writer. It was all I knew. I could write pages and pages and at the time I was writing jokes. I loved watching stand-up and was enthralled by American comics.

I plucked up the courage and asked Steve, 'Could you connect me with one of your clients for me to show them a writing sample?'

Steve recommended I got in touch with the editor of

---

* Annoying acronym for Black, Asian and Minority Ethnic, which ironically ethnic minorities don't enjoy. Surprise.

the bank's in-house magazine. I did and she connected me with a comedian, Lucy. She told me it was entirely up to the comedian whether she had the time and inclination to indulge me.

I sent the comedian an email asking her if she could look at some of my material. She trumped my offer by suggesting that we could meet up. I was overjoyed! I'd never met a comedian before and wondered if it was a small community where everyone looked out for one another. Did she have Chris Rock on speed dial? Could she arrange an introduction? I didn't know what would happen if I met him, I just knew it would be funny.

We met at an American diner near her house. She was a beautiful woman, full of life. One of the first things she said to me was, 'We need to have more diversity in comedy.' She had just seen *Sex and the City 2* and wasn't pleased with the way it appropriated Arabian culture. I didn't really know any posh white women like her, so I tried not to judge. I saw that it was well meaning, yet odd. I put it down to the popular trend at the time to be 'allies', or at least to see us.

At the time, I had no knowledge of what the comedy industry was, let alone my place in it. I had been working at various establishments trying to figure out what I wanted to do and attempting not to get married off. This statement from her threw me into the politics of the comedy industry before I fully understood the world for myself. I wasn't to know how the machine operated and so without being able to see this for myself it was hard to know which came first – was I excluded or did I feel excluded as a placebo effect because that's what *she* told me to expect?

She said she couldn't help me be a writer, but after looking at my work she remarked, 'These are jokes. You should be a comedian.'

I chuckled awkwardly. 'Um, I have thought about that but I'm too afraid. I don't think I could stand up in front of people ...'

She said, 'You don't know any of the people in the room. If you don't like it once you've tried it, you walk out of there and you never have to see them again.'

'I can't, it's so scary,' I protested, taking a sip of my water.

She looked at me intently. 'Listen, you can try it once, or you can spend the rest of your life wondering what if. Even if you do it once, think of what an exciting story it will be to tell your grandchildren. Most people just sit indoors watching *X-Factor*. I may not have the time to do those things, but I'm fulfilling my life with better things. It's a privilege to have people listen to you.'

I couldn't say no to her, and I felt it might be worth pushing myself. 'Maybe in six months?' I said non-committally.

She shook her head. 'You need to have a deadline, otherwise it'll get too big in your head.'

Right there at the table she picked up her phone

and called a friend and got me a gig. I couldn't quite believe what was happening.

She smiled at me. 'Right, you've got a gig in two weeks' time, in Regent's Park. It won't be a pub crowd who will be a bit taken aback by you, it'll be a lovely supportive female crowd.'

I didn't process what she meant by the reaction she anticipated from the pub crowd. I knew I could make people laugh but things were happening so fast. One minute I was meeting a comedian for a chat about writing, the next minute I was about to perform stand-up.

As she opened my manuscript she said, 'I know that it's hard when someone reads your writing for the first time, it's like being naked.' This instantly put me at ease. Even though I had only just met her, she got it. She looked at what I'd written about my time working in a call centre and said, 'Ha! That's funny. I'll help you tighten it up. You can come to my flat next week and do a rehearsal.'

I didn't know what to say. 'Oh my God, OK!'

I may not have had the courage to ask her for Chris Rock's number, but I certainly got more help from her than I'd expected.

I remember panicking so much beforehand. What if I forgot my lines? That was all I could think about. I went around her flat the following week. It was difficult to perform initially but I eased into it as she made me feel comfortable. I told her I was worried about forgetting my lines.

'It's fine if you read from the page. In my sets I tend to walk to my table and while I have a drink of water I'll glance at my notes. It's a good trick as it reminds me of my lines and leaves the audience wanting more too.'

My mind was blown, this was such good insider information!

After my first full run-through, the first thing that she corrected me on was my body language. I had my legs crossed and was standing very awkwardly.

'Sadia,' she looked at me knowingly. 'When we were in the savannah* we had to appear confident so that lions wouldn't come and eat us.'

I looked confused and worried where this might go. I definitely hadn't read or been informed about any good part in history where white people were in Africa.

'It is all about confidence,' she clarified.

Apparently, if I looked confident the audience would automatically feel at ease around me. Whereas if I looked nervous, that would transfer to them. She told me to stand with one foot forward.

---

* White people start talking about savannahs as a reference to pre-historic times. They're talking about an African ecosystem. I usually smile and nod a lot during these conversations as it can go off on a tangent quite a lot.

I was mega self-conscious about it all, but as I uncrossed my legs and put one leg forward, I automatically felt more confident. I marked my territory and firmly stood my ground. I thought of how Chris Rock had prowled the stage in his leather suit in the HBO comedy special, *Bigger and Blacker*. I knew I was ready for the challenge; I just had to stand like I belonged there.

The two weeks flew by. Before I knew it, there I was standing outside of the venue in Regent's Park, a grand town building made of white bricks. I was more anxious than I had been at any other point in my life. The material was prepped, and I had a cue card with bullet points in case I lost my bearings. I went to the backstage area and met the other acts. Quite a few of the other female acts were performing for their first time too, which was comforting. We collectively went to the girls bathroom to gather ourselves and get ready to hit the stage. After we'd taken a minute to pull ourselves together, I saw I had a missed call from Lucy.

I texted her:

> Sorry me and the girls went to the loo – so nervous. We're backstage.

I went through my routine repeatedly in my head. I tried to understand why people did this for a living, it seemed like I was setting myself up for a massive fall – either that or I was about to have a heart attack. I tried to think about all the things Lucy taught me.

Pause.

Breathe.

Stand with one leg forward.

Drink water.

Eventually Lucy arrived and we hugged.

She looked thoughtful and said, 'When you texted me, I only saw the beginning part of the message and I thought you were saying sorry because you weren't going through with it, and I had just hopped into the cab here. But then when I saw you said you were all nervous, I laughed because that's such a thing a comedian would say! You're going to be great.' I sensed her supportive vibes and felt humbled and encouraged. It meant so much to me since I hadn't told anyone about this, not even my folks or friends.

And then suddenly it was my turn. I walked on to the stage and I was taken aback by how easy it felt. I had not allowed for adrenaline either – and what a rush it was. When I got my first big laugh my right knee started to shake – something that had never happened to me before or since.* I finished the rest of my set and received my first ever applause. As I walked off the stage, I was filled with happiness, I had just done my first gig! In the interval an elderly Indian woman

---

* Who knew comedy turned you into Elvis?

came and gave me her card and said I should get in touch as she wanted to book me for a gig.

Lucy and I went out for dinner afterwards. She congratulated me on the night. I didn't want that night to ever end. I felt so whole. We sat outside a nearby restaurant, and we were joined by a successful Asian comedian. She seemed taken aback by me, a hijabi, as there wasn't a lot of diversity on the circuit, let alone Muslim acts. Lucy and this comedian talked a little shop about the challenges in the industry, and to be honest half of it went over my head and the other half of me was having an out-of-body experience from all the adrenaline. I felt like a drug addict coming off a high. It couldn't have gone any better. I had made an entire crowd of people laugh and nothing had ever felt so good.

The Asian comic didn't stay for long, but before she ventured off she seemed almost slighted, and remarked, 'Comedy's all about attitude.'

Lucy seemed surprised by the fact that she hadn't seemed very interested in the new up-and-coming Asian talent sat right in front of her and commented, 'I had hoped she would take you under her wing.'

That hadn't surprised me, I know perfectly well that the concept of community cohesion among Asians is often just aesthetics. From the comedian's perspective, she was the diversity, so it would be doing her no favours to open doors for the rest. Perhaps a part of her felt that because she had to figure it out for herself, so should everyone else.

The thing that surprised me, that I hadn't realised before, was that I didn't want the Asian comedian as a mentor. When Lucy suggested it, I knew I preferred her. She said, 'Don't worry, I'll figure it out. I'm always here to help.'

I knew what had happened tonight was almost certainly too good to be true and asked tentatively, 'What about the gigs that don't go well?'*

In her typically upbeat style and with a bright smile she reassuringly replied, 'You'll just have more stories to tell.'

I'm an Asian, but I don't like to play into stereotypes, so I thought rather than work in IT I'd get a job in a call centre. This is what a typical day was like for me:

'Hello, you're through to Sadia. How may I help?'

'Sandra?'

'No, Sadia.'

'Claudia?'

'No, it's still Sadia.'

'That's a funny name.'

'It's Indian.'

'You don't sound very Indian.'

'That's cos I was born in Essex.'

---

* The technical term is dying and, yes, it is *every* bit as bad as it sounds.

'You're not in India now, are you?'

'No, I'm in London.'

'Good, I hate Indian call centres. They're so stupid and I never understand a word they're saying.'

'Yes, sir, that must be very frustrating for you.'

You have to say that part because the inbound calls are recorded, but later when I got a break, I called that man back.

In an Indian accent: 'Hello, I'm calling you from India, where all the call centre staff have gathered together to award you a prize!'

'Really? What have I won?'

'We voted you motherfucker of the month!'

The outbound calls aren't recorded.

I continued behind the scenes in comedy in the same way I was 'back office' in the call centre. I randomly got asked to be in a BBC short called *My Jihad* at one point, as a background artist at an Asian wedding. In typical style, I said yes without knowing what a background artist was and assumed it was the same thing as being an actor. As this was my first ever time on set, I had no idea what to expect. I have to say, when I showed up, I was expecting it to be a bigger part!*

After travelling halfway across London to location, near Uxbridge, I arrived at 10 a.m. and was shown

---

* My biggest role to date was Tree Number Three in my school play.

into a large room where I was placed with about fifty other background artists. I was so grateful I had done my own make-up as I discovered they were not doing any for the extras.

The room looked like a mix between an airport lounge and backstage at a fashion show. Everyone had brought along bags and suitcases – as we'd been asked to bring a few options of clothing. I hadn't bothered as I liked my outfit, plus I had on my shiny black-and-white sparkly hijab which I knew was a winner. The likelihood was we wouldn't make the final cut, so it was weird to me that the other background artists were making such a fuss given how inconsequential our parts were. I didn't realise it at the time – it was this level of commitment that was required to progress in this industry.

It is eye-opening how unglamourous the so-called 'show' business industry is. We sat around in a room all day like we were in quarantine, me and the other extras, chewing gum and blowing bubbles. Every few hours, someone had the fortitude to get up and find one of the people running around with a clipboard to see if there was any information on when we would be released.

I made small talk with a few of the other background artists and they all asked the same thing: 'Who are you with?' I wasn't with a casting agency at the time, so I just replied, 'The BBC.' Many of them told me the details of their casting agencies and I made a note on my phone to follow up.

Suddenly, after what felt like hours of waiting, a white woman came in and uttered the golden words to the room, 'You're needed on set in five.' The room that had felt so quiet beforehand broke out into what felt like a loud and unruly scene in *America's Next Top Model*. Everyone ran in the direction of the full-length mirrors to adjust our hair and hijabs, make-up and general looks. We went to set at 8 p.m., but the excitement was short-lived as being there was yet another test of patience. We did the same scene repeatedly until someone decided enough was enough.

I was wearing a tight black top that kept creeping up ever so slightly. It was surreal when a white production assistant would come and tug it down to preserve my modesty between takes. In this moment, individual preference about how my clothing fell didn't matter. They wanted to strike the right Asian tone, and this was a pointed reminder that I was not it.

I did manage to get a line, though,* where I said, 'How much do you earn?'

I had tried to sign up to the well-known Asian artists agency that had been recommended, but they rejected my application as they had enough Asians on the books. A few months later though, I managed

---

* This earned me an extra £25.

to sign up with a new extra's agency. I was trying to make it and this felt like a step in the right direction. I did odd jobs when I could to make a bit of money. Though it takes a special type of person to get being an extra wrong somehow, I managed it. I kept walking 'too close' to Sir Ian McKellan on the set of *The Good Liar* and was politely requested to 'keep out of his way' by the production crew.

Comedy, TV and media was a strange world that I was beginning to get used to. There was often a lot of waiting between jobs and you'd grab them as soon as they came up, no matter how small they were. I would get a lot of time to talk to people doing extra work during the long days and waiting around, people from all backgrounds, industries and walks of life. The thing that we all had in common was that we wanted to 'make it'. Although what this meant was distinctly undefined – the only thing I could be certain of was this *wasn't* it.

Things I never knew I needed to know about white people:

- ♡ Their mother or father has spent time in India and helped liberate the movement.
- ♡ White people get their news from and listen to Radio 4. You're nobody if you don't participate.

- ♡ White people use alcohol to mask their problems and insecurities.
- ♡ How wasted, high, intoxicated they are against their current record.
- ♡ White people think you're insane if you don't believe in evolution.
- ♡ White guilt is for them and not about you. It helps them feel like they're not completely void of emotion despite the fact it changes nothing.*
- ♡ They're crazy about dogs and cats and we'll never know why.
- ♡ They can't believe Muslims go without bacon.
- ♡ They say 'You're oppressed' but also 'When are you going to get married?'

---

* It's also not a healthy state to be in, let alone a character trait.

9

Training Day

I met Ray J at a gym I joined to lose some weight while I was trying to kick off my career as comedian/extra/writer. He was a personal trainer. I knew from the start he wasn't into me; instead he gave off the impression that he merely tolerated me. Sadly, that's what attracted me to him most. He would roll his eyes at me so petulantly, I *liked* that he didn't like me. I didn't need him to. I liked him enough for the both of us. He was gorgeous. He was Asian, dark-haired and had the longest eyelashes. I liked his voice a lot, commanding and deep.

I mainly just stared at him every time I went to the gym, it was the only thing that made me build up a sweat and I'm sure the only calories I lost were from all the pent-up sexual energy. He was so handsome in a way that almost seemed unreal, and he had a great body. I liked every outfit he wore; I don't know if that was a coincidence. I knew I wanted him as soon as I saw him. He was the most beautiful man who had ever spoken to me in real life. He was so out of my league it went to my head. I had none of my senses when he was around, and it was a shame, as I think subtlety was up his street. He was one of those guys that knew how pretty he was and so was very particular about who he associated with.

One time, he offered to give me a lift home and told me not to get the wrong idea. I had no idea what the right or the wrong idea was. I managed to calm down, although I had been really nervous being in a fit guy's car. He knocked the gearstick against my knee accidentally on purpose. I flirted back, 'Be careful, I need my knees strong when I'm giving head'. He acted surprised; however, he was always talking about sex. He would confide in me like I was one of the boys, 'I'm on to a promise Saturday night.' I wasn't sure whether he was bragging or trying to make me jealous, probably both. When I asked him why everything to him was about sex, he answered, 'Who doesn't like sex?' I guess he had a point – I mean, I've even written a book about it now.

I got his number and I texted him whenever I could find something to say. He would reply but there was nothing to suggest that there was any interest on his side. I did anything to get his attention, but nothing worked. Once I turned up to the gym in a dark purple, ruched mini-dress and he ignored me the whole time.

It only made me want him more.

At times, his indifference towards me shifted to flirting, like when he would grab my wrist to smell my perfume, though I couldn't tell if he was developing feels or whether he was just flattered by my attention. He was always non-committal. He'd text:

I don't do nondescript relationships.

I was just so impressed by his vocabulary. He was an English lit graduate, and I loved that he was in touch with his sensitive side. Ray J sniffed out early on that I was a virgin. For that reason, and also because he didn't want anything heavy, he refused to be my boyfriend – rude, I know.

'I don't have sex with virgins,' he would declare whenever I'd hint at wanting a relationship.* I got the feeling he wanted to keep his options open and would have been open to me if I was less hassle. And because I couldn't have him, I wanted him ten times over.

I didn't always have time for a workout, but I really enjoyed chatting with him and sometimes I'd bring him lunch as an excuse to see him. I'd drop by with sushi from Prêt and he'd complain it wasn't cold and that

---

* This went against everything I knew, was taught and believed. Up until this point I had understood that this was all a man ever wanted.

warm sushi could 'kill him'. Once he held my hand and placed it on his six-pack, I swear I died, before quickly moving it away too soon. At the same time he was accusing *me* of being the tease.

We used to text each other every night and it was on one of these nights that he completely changed his tune, informing me he'd decided that we were going to have sex or we'd have to go our separate ways.

It wasn't long after this that we had our first kiss. It was unexpected. We were stood outside in the dark as he was closing the gym. It was November and he was wearing a white jumper that hugged him so tightly that I wished I was the jumper. Out of nowhere he kissed me, and I felt so many emotions fill me up. It's what I'd wanted for so long – his desire – and I couldn't believe my persistence had worked. I pulled back and he leaned in again. He pressed his hand against my left cheek as he kissed me deeper. It was like being in a fairy tale, even if in this one it was the princess chasing the prince. I softened in his arms, affirming to myself that he was 'The One'.

'I could eat you with a spoon,' he said. He was also a really good kisser, and I felt proud that I was too, given I hadn't had any tutorials. I'd never even practised on my arm. It meant so much to me, that kiss, especially as I had been overlooked by guys for so long. It felt like I'd found all the things I'd been looking for. I was so turned on and I wanted us to carry on but we couldn't outside.

Due to my inexperience, I didn't know what any of this meant. Were we seeing each other now? Did he like me? Was this for keeps? I couldn't bring myself to ask any of these questions for fear of it ending the moment I'd tried so long to create with him.

In the following weeks, there was a lot of back and forth. I sexted him a lot to show willing. To this day I think I was better at sexting when I was a virgin – I had an endless arsenal of filthy innuendos – literal sex bombs. What I lacked in form, I made up for in zeal.

> I can make you rock hard all night.

> Let's do it in the shower, you made me so wet.

> Will you fuck me three times tomorrow?

Sometimes I'd sense incredulity on his part, but it only made me more determined.

I was keen to meet him somewhere to pick up where we left off that evening, but he seemed to get cold feet. We set a date to meet only for him to cancel at the last minute. He apologised without having any excuse and I was hurt at being messed around. He said he would make it up to me but he never did.

Despite him never giving me what I wanted, I couldn't get him out of my mind and I believed him when he said he would make it up to me. It was only a week after this that Ray J took me back to his friend's flat. Our first kiss had been so special that I had really high expectations for every physical encounter going forward. Surely that was only the beginning? That evening he hurried me up the stairs and as we got inside the room, I noticed someone had been painting. He said he'd been decorating which turned me on. He pulled down my hijab in the bedroom as we were making out. Once it came off, he whispered to me, 'I think I prefer you with it on.' A foolish part of me thought if he saw my hair it might have meant something. He knew that, but he never made it feel like a stand-out moment.

I ignored his comment and we carried on kissing. It wasn't the same as the first time. He had been warm and considerate then and made me feel special. This time, we felt less connected. He was moving fast, and I didn't get the urgency. It was my first time so more than anything I wanted to take it slow, not pressured. This was compounded by the fact that we hadn't discussed what we were to one another or what we wanted. There was no healthy communication between us, just a hunger to be close to each other – romantic on my side, animalistic on his. It felt like although things were advancing physically, emotionally we wanted different things.

We wanted to get down and have sex, but I had a problem with being fingered that I didn't know I had beforehand. Every time he put his hand there, I had to move it away. I'm not sure what this was. I would have been completely fine with anything else but there was something about his hand that made me feel on edge. I think it hurt his ego as he mistook this for a disinterest in him, even though I couldn't have shown him any more interest. He expected me to prove it to him, without proving any loyalty to me himself. He looked at me exasperatedly and sighed. 'Have a drink. It'll loosen you up.' I must have looked confused, he knew I didn't drink so it really wasn't a helpful or viable suggestion.

I tried to kiss his mouth, but he would never let me. The rare times he met my lips was when he chose to, he was always in control. He was like Julia Roberts in *Pretty Woman* except irritating.

'Women fall in love with me,' he warned me and he would push his face away or scrunch his lips out to prevent mine from meeting his. 'It'll make me cum, don't,' he complained. I'd never come across this sort of attitude in my life, there isn't even a porn category for it, but at the same time I didn't feel I deserved any better. I really wanted him and so it was on his terms.

As he got handsy, I tried initiating dirty talk the way I'd seen in films, and so I said in my best sexy voice, 'What you doing?' as I ran my hands down his big arms.

Out of the blue he threw a temper tantrum, pushing me away and shouting, 'If you don't wanna play, get out of the playground!'

I stood back feeling shaken and upset. I didn't know how he could misconstrue what I said so badly.

He grabbed his jacket and called to me as he opened the door, 'Come on, let's go, I'll take you home.'

I didn't know what I'd done wrong, I was stunned, it felt like we had barely started. I had trusted he knew what he was doing – being older and the expert on sex and all. Of all the ways I'd pictured the night ending, I couldn't have imagined it would be like this.

I sensed that he was super aware of his conscience around me, like he felt guilt, and it had put him off. He expected me to be instantly up for it without any effort on his part. So, I pulled myself together and followed him out the door.

Ray J's deliberate and unfiltered comments made it so difficult to let go and relax around him. I spent our time together never knowing who he was, or what this 'connection' we had was. He was there but also expressly unavailable and, being a novice, it was far too much to comprehend amid my intense feelings for him. The whole exchange revolved around him and what he wanted. I was so desperate for his acceptance that I willingly surrendered myself to him.

My experiences with Ray J would go on to shape what I felt I deserved from a man – and sadly, that was next to nothing. He made me obsessed with wanting to be good in bed, which is where I placed all my worth. I thought that to be a sex bomb I had to prove myself in this relationship against all odds. All my vows to not lose my head or go crazy over the opposite sex fell to the wayside and, like many women before me, I fell into a toxic relationship that hoovered up all my energy and left me feeling empty. The emptiness was a cavernous void, only filled by mutual love and respect, something I would never get from Ray J no matter how hard I tried.

10

Broken English

It was the age of acquisitions and mergers. Currys swallowed up Dixons. Arcadia united with Topshop. Co-op bought Somerfield. The Bank of Scotland joined Lloyds. Orange and T-Mobile even got married. But I was still on the shelf.

Long before Emma Watson declared she was dating herself, young Asian girls like me were in relationships with ourselves. It wasn't a trend, a phase or even a choice, it was simply a reality. Clearly this wasn't what I, or any rational-minded individual, would want, rather it was down to my circumstances. Part of them being that Ray J was a total fuckboi who would never acknowledge me beyond what suited him.

Despite my lack of meaningful relationships, a man

had been a part of my story before I'd even been on a date. As an Asian woman, my association to men is apparently tattooed on my forehead. The sheer prospect of a man in my life was titillating to strangers, who were certain my family had my affairs covered, without having any idea or interest in my circumstances. People make the assumption I'm spoken for before I've even opened my mouth. And they weren't totally wrong because as an Asian woman my whole life *should* have been about weddings, but instead of hopping between wedding shops I was hopping between jobs.

The only attention I got in my teenage years, and I'm sure many Asian women have suffered the same, was unwanted attention from uncles. Not sugar daddies, just daddies or granddaddies. That is enough to give me the ick forever. These old perverts would size me up like I was their next meal and it didn't do much for my self-esteem in my teens knowing that the guys who liked me were sixty-year-old unattractive freshies.* By the time I was twenty-three, they had moved on. But from this point all I attracted were looks of pity from these men and others as they wondered 'what had gone wrong' for me to still be on the market.

I hadn't wanted to become bitter, but my long virginal stance was burning a hole in my knickers. I was told my virginity would be glowingly virtuous but

---

* People from India/Pakistan who are 'fresh off the boat'.

actually it was an invisible plight. If I advertised it, I'd be saying I was inexperienced and bad at sex, and with the rise of films like *The 40-year-old Virgin*, it started to feel like a disease for the socially awkward. I was scared about what I would become. I might have been saving myself some heartache and painful STIs but it felt like if I held on to my virginity for any longer, I'd never be able to get rid of it. My overthinking comes from the way piety and chastity were constantly instilled in me growing up. It made me overrate the value of my pussy in relation to its market value. It made the whole act a huge thing when really, it wasn't at all. I spent some of my best years on a self-imposed vaginal exile.

Was my honour really up my vagina? Or was it in my character and how I conducted my affairs?

One of the concerns I held was that the tightness of my pussy would be collateral damage to losing my virginity. Since tight pussy was highly sought after, this made me reluctant to give it up. Obviously now I know that having loads of sex does not 'stretch' or 'widen' your pussy, but back then this myth made its way into my psyche and bothered me. It's crazy that even though this wasn't based on an actual conversation with anyone in my life, I was still privy to this ill-advised information. Eventually, I learnt that dicks shouldn't be given the glory of suggesting they could 'widen' a vagina – they really aren't that impressive – and honestly, have you seen the size of some of them?

Ray J was blowing hot and cold, and we still hadn't had sex despite the fact he'd continually say that's all he wanted. He was hot if we had no plans and would bump into each other casually, and cold if I suggested doing things that couples do. I'd ask him to go out for a coffee, go to the movies or for a walk in the park and he would say no without hesitation. He was prepared to be a part of my life under very specific conditions, which undermined the fact that he was in my life at all. I wanted to do nice things, but often the choice was doing it by myself or not at all. I had no one to share experiences like sunsets, sightseeing or fine dining with, so often it was easier to deny myself these experiences. I worked long and fixed shifts, so it was hard to coordinate with friends who did the same. I still bought two tickets for everything, but no guy magically appeared to go with me as I had half hoped they would.

The only exception I made was for comedy, that was my own thing and something I was trying to learn more and more about as I continued doing my irregular stand-up gigs. I remember being the only Brown person standing in a long queue outside Leicester Square Theatre. I was in search of funny and I had received good information that Mike Birbiglia was it. I sat through the whole show unamused. He was perfectly nice but none of what he said made me laugh, his comedy just isn't for me and that is completely fine.

The next comedian I went to see was Eddie Griffin. It was right after Michael Jackson died and so Eddie clearly wasn't sticking to the script. He was grieving his pal and it wasn't a show at all. He drank and drank and tried to right the wrongs of the persecution Michael Jackson suffered; his pain was palpable through the comedy. In trying to convince us how great his pal was he told us his late friend had a 'titanic of a dick'. Other than one routine towards the end, the show was a complete write-off. I made the long journey back in the cold and dark to East London, alone. It lingered with me, whether a good show was about being present in the here and now, raw, authentic and spontaneous. Or whether it was about being good at delivering tried and tested punchlines and getting laughs. The reality is it was probably both.

Then I saw that Chris Rock was coming to the UK! I booked a ticket online straight away. I even remember the seat was F17, which was close and central enough. I hoped I might be able to meet with him after the show and get some words of wisdom for my pursuit of comedy.

That evening when I arrived at Hammersmith Apollo, however, the venue told me that it wouldn't be possible to meet him. I couldn't find any contact details online for him and so I was completely at their mercy. The nice lady in the ticket booth looked at me with empathy after I passed her my fan mail and a cuddly toy I had got him from Clinton Cards. She said she would try her best to see if she could pass it on for me. She took my personal details and address in case he wanted to write back, and I thanked her for being so kind.

I'm almost glad I didn't meet him then because I have no idea what I would have done. I was willing to risk it all for that man. To me, he is comedy incarnate.

Most of my time would be spent alone, in my thoughts or trying to escape them. I didn't trust people very easily and so shut myself off from them in self-protection. I was taught to be cautious of having fun, and so I didn't do much of that. I was always encouraged to focus on work and that I should be mindful of people meddling in my affairs, and so I did just that. You'd think comedy requires someone to be the total opposite of this but really, it's a very lonely career. You perform for an audience, but true connections can often elude you. I liked being in control of what people saw in me, I wanted them to see a funny and confident Sadia, and make them laugh. I kept the other more vulnerable Sadia buried inside me. The trouble with this guardedness was that sheltering myself and leaning into my comfort zones left me inexperienced and missing out on essential life lessons. I was falling behind and wasn't sure how to catch up.

I still knew that my chances of finding a man to marry by this point were low given that at twenty-three, I was considered past it. Asian women are normally married and well into the throes of family life by my age. I had a small hope that I might be wrong but, having no social life, was conscious that there were few opportunities for me to find one. Also, besotted as I was with Ray J, I was in the unenviable position of neither being in or out of a relationship. Besides, I was too stubborn to go and look for a man myself, and so I put my focus and energy into writing and comedy in the hours when I wasn't working.

I wasn't really into social media. People posting pictures of their breakfast and cats had no appeal for me, so it was with great reluctance that I joined Facebook, fashionably late. Without it I was practically invisible as a comedian.

My Facebook account did something unexpected and unappealing – it attracted messages from all sorts of strange men. Specifically Asian men based overseas, mainly in Pakistan and India. Guys with 'MD MD' in their titles. The more qualifications they posted in their bio the less I trusted them. This was an unleashing of a whole new horror, the pool of men who wanted me also wanted visas and passports. It became even more confusing to try and ascertain what would be in it for me, or if they were interested in me at all. Their lack of etiquette with the ladies was blatant from the brief and often nonsensical messages they would send like:

> Hye

> +9178656745676

> Call me

To add to the confusion, some of these men would have pictures of women on their avatars, maybe in a way to placate the person they were openly trying to catfish. Some had pictures of kids and looked like they might even be married. When, out of sheer curiosity, I glanced through their Facebook profiles at their friends, I was even more stunned that most of the people they followed were called Sadia. They had programmed an algorithm to connect with all the Sadias!

This was not the reach I wanted. A lot of these guys were trying to marry me for all the wrong reasons, like my name, without even knowing me. The fact that they thought they had a chance was not easy to live down. Though I wanted a man, it made me feel even more isolated and compelled me to stay clear of the dating scene as I didn't want to stumble across the wrong sort. My merger with the male species would have to wait.

11

Green Book

It was a sticky-hot day in early June and I was waiting on Edgware Road to be picked up for a conservative Asian comedy gig. Though I had been in the game four years at this point, I didn't have a clue what this event might entail, and not even Lucy could help me on this one. When the organisers showed, they asked if they could put me in a different vehicle to the male performers. Not wanting to cause a scene, I said fine, though it would mean spending the four-hour drive on my own. None of the male comedians spoke out for me to travel with them though there was space in their six-seater. Genders are encouraged not to mix in Islam and this gave the male Asian comedians an inherent reason not to associate with me. It didn't matter how isolated or lonely this made me feel, it was the rules.

As if this wasn't enough, I then opened the passenger door to the vehicle I was ushered towards and the driver (male) asked me to sit in the backseat so I wouldn't be sitting next to him. I was annoyed and sulked in the backseat the whole way. As a comedian I already felt like an outsider, but feeling like one among my own community was not something I'd expected.

At the time my act was more tame, but given how few female Muslim acts there were – you could literally count them on one hand – I was still considered a little provocative. Many Asian comedians signalled their disapproval by distancing themselves from me and showed their hypocrisy by condoning the same content from non-Muslim female acts. They just pretended I did not exist.

Comedy is strange in that it almost works as a microcosm of wider society. It's a mini society where if you are a cis, white heterosexual man you are more likely to be on the top, and if you are anything else, you have to work so much harder. The more successful an Asian comedian got, the more they were able to distance themselves from up-and-coming Asian acts, date a white woman and crucially lament on how difficult it was being an Asian act – despite their progression. They took every opportunity to play the race card to further their career despite preferring to fraternise with white comedians both professionally and personally, where they could. This was something they kept private and did not want to draw attention to – but it only goes to show how in control of the industry white males are, that these men would do anything to get close to them so they could also claw their way to the top.

It made it harder for me to embrace these Asian comedians as they were always trying to get acceptance, rather than to be funny. I was left uninspired by them as it felt like they were pandering to white people and over-egging a plight that wasn't totally their experience. Audiences would fetishise ethnic comedians who sought their acceptance, and to me this wasn't comedy but some other obsequious nonsense. The way these acts would focus on their difficult experiences often felt like making themselves the butt of the joke and to me this was both a poor use of the art form and of their voices.

I felt audiences, particularly Asian audiences, deserved so much more than a one-sided narrative about being disenfranchised. Asian audiences deserved to be entertained like any other, not just reminded of, and at times inflamed by, the microaggressions we could be prone to. That's why there's a huge lack of diverse and inspiring Asian role models.* It's systemic not by accident – the

---

* The comedians that made sense on stage didn't make any sense off stage and vice versa. For example, Bill Cosby – squeaky-clean onstage but offstage it's a different story.

ones with platforms are the ones who speak about racism and themselves in relation to white people for their comedy. The reason it's awful is because everyone takes what they say to be the truth and so think it's the same for everyone, when everyone's stories are different. While these comedians succeeded commercially, they lacked artistic merit. Comedy for me was about playing from my heart and my truth, not to speak for my race but about my own experiences.

I found comedy quite challenging in the beginning. None of my peers really wanted me in comedy and this made it tough especially when I already lacked self-belief. For so long I've felt like an inconvenience in the industry. From the way I was dismissed, just like when I was put into a separate car on the way to that gig, I got the impression that most of these comedians thought or hoped comedy was a phase for me until I got married and then I would just disappear. Ha! Little did they know I had no luck on the marriage front! It was hard to know at times whether I was being rejected because of my race, gender or because I was new. I hoped it wasn't because my jokes were bad, but you never know.

I suffered a double dose of innate self-loathing as an Asian and a comedian. I had a subconscious racial self-hatred, and the more I uncovered through self-reflection in comedy, the more it made me hate myself all over again. Even when people were kind or complimentary it meant nothing when my own feelings about myself were so low. I didn't believe anyone and just thought they had some ulterior motive. I grew so used to the bad that I couldn't stomach the good.

I remember during a conversation with one Asian comedian, she said she would send me some contacts for writing agents, but she never did. It felt weird that Lucy was happy to help but Asian acts acted so miserly – I mean, what were they going to lose? It was like being in nursery, and no one wanted to share. One of the unspoken rules I learnt early on was not to try and be funny around other comedians. I was duly informed that this could piss off comedians who didn't want to feel upstaged, and if I did this, I could get a reputation for being a dickhead. I was baffled, *for doing my job? Something I loved?* I just didn't get it. The more I found out, the more I realised it was less about being funny, and more about being neurotic. Over time it dawned on me that the comedy world wasn't the small-knit community I had believed it would be where everyone vouched for one another. It was every (wo)man an island. And the island was like the one in *Lost* – scary and unforgiving.

I went to several gigs where specifically female comedians ignored me. One was a charity gig where a famous comedian was headlining who, when I smiled, refused to make eye contact, as if to say she was better than me. At another gig a well-known comedian didn't say hello or good luck, her only words to me were, 'You've lost a lot of weight.'

Everything I represented was threatening. As a card-carrying hijabi, it gave me the potential ability to punch up and so you could say I had an edge (little did they know I'd be trying to punch up through tempered glass). Instead of embracing me, and the things I had to offer, they ostracised me, even though they were using their sexuality, gender and any other means to succeed as part of their act. My visible lack of privilege was what made me a threat – competitively speaking.*
When it came to some audiences, a few asked me if I wore my headscarf 'as part of my act'. Comedy could be political but I had worn the scarf long before getting into comedy and wasn't using it as a stunt.

It's partly these experiences that make it difficult for me to embrace everyday feminism, as my experiences are not in line with most women. Feminism gives me a false sense of security that all women are well-intentioned and part of a 'sisterhood'. This is not how things worked in real terms, as in we comedians find ourselves competing against one another. At times it feels surreal, as the concept of feminism feels more important to women than the way we treat each other in real life. I also made some friends with women and

---

* Never play the game 'who's got it worst' with white people – no good can come of it.

men of colour, but sadly it was fleeting and there were fewer connections than I'd have liked.

I learnt to find friends in unexpected places, among them were a few straight white males in the industry and a handful of white women not far behind. For instance, my good mates and comedians Stu Laws and Annie McGrath would ask me to do gigs and be in sketches. They made the industry the most accessible for me and showed their priority towards diversity through helping Black, Asian and other ethnicity acts as much as possible. It filled me up with joy when they went out of their way, especially when there was no incentive other than the act itself. What they showed was they had really educated themselves and tried to look beyond our differences. This was evident from our conversations where there was a genuine interest and also sensitivity to subject matters, acknowledging their privilege without belittling me. There was a sense that they appreciated some of the challenges I might have faced and gave me gigs and lifts to gigs, and an ear to be honest after a difficult show, neither judging nor pitying me.

This helped me appreciate the richness in diversity and how things were sometimes different from the narrative I was led to expect. I would have expected Asians to be allies by default, when in fact, this was often too much to ask. I would have expected nothing from white male comedians and yet they were quite generous in including me, in many cases for no reason other than to support me in gaining experience or a credit.

The more I tried to break through, the more I saw I didn't fit into any of the established circuits. There was something called the 'alternative' comedy scene, which sounded appealing except it was full of middle-class, white and/or rich Oxbridge-educated acts. Only in England could both the mainstream and the alternative circuits be this monotheistic! Some of these acts were even masquerading as lowly arts types. It was staggering to see some of these elitist acts complaining about how poor they were to sell their DVDs. Even white, working-class comics were astonished given they had no idea what poor was compared to an actual working-class experience.

Then there was the art circuit, which was basically a set of arts centre venues, and eventually I saw I didn't fit in there either. I approached a fancy one in the suburbs to perform, and the lady liked the 'look' of me but said I was too 'vulgar'. She said that my material wouldn't resonate with her audiences, and if I could not swear, just smile and tap dance then she could think about it. But that wasn't comedy and just because I wasn't the correct kind of 'vulgar' or 'sexual' to suit her didn't mean I couldn't make people laugh. I wanted to tell it how it is. I wanted to joke about the things that made me – and many other Asian and working-class people – laugh, but it seemed these were the very same things that made some of their middle-class audiences shudder. It made their masks slip and exposed them. It fed them the reality of the world, which was bitter and hard to swallow. What they wanted was a sweet-tasting appeasement cake.

The longer I spent in the industry, the more I learnt that it wasn't about being funny, it was hierarchical and about being in circles of influence, amassing power and holding on to it. My biggest problem was that often I was on my own, where I felt safest, whereas my colleagues were networking, drinking and making sure everyone knew who they were. I didn't want to be part of the mess and chaos, and being the extro-verted, loud person wasn't intrinsic to my personality. Most of these ultra-loud, out-there people were being so to hide insecurity and self-doubt. I didn't need to pretend or fake friendships with people to hide the hurt. It was always there with me, and I preferred to keep that low-key and private.

Eventually I realised that my place was nowhere and I didn't fit in.

It was easier to embrace that than to resist it.

12

The Last King of Scotland

When I became a comedian, I heard of something called the Edinburgh Fringe Festival, also known as the world's largest arts festival. It's a festival where comedians meticulously plan to showcase their material and more importantly, endeavour to become famous overnight. The artists, predominantly based in and around London, plus the industry (producers, commissioners, agents and talent scouts), also largely based in London and the surrounding areas, have an unspoken pact that instead of meeting locally any time of the year, they should spend the month of August in a cold, rainier climate. The anticipation and promise of Edinburgh is enough of a reason for these two groups not to meet up outside the city the other eleven months out of the year.

For me it was a trade fair where I hoped for five-star reviews and to consort with A-list/TV comics, but the reality of flyering in the rain, navigating crowds where nobody recognised me and reflecting on how I would never be as famous as the official drink of Scotland, a deep, fizzy orange soda called Irn-Bru, brought me painfully down to earth. If you hadn't purchased X number of life-sized billboards and placards before arriving, then what were you even doing there? I felt like I'd been scammed but it is also the reality of being a comedian. I'd spent money on rent, marketing, publicity, venues, directors, advertising and that was before I'd even arrived.

I first did the festival in 2011 when I was twenty-four with my show *Please Hold, You're Being Transferred To A UK-Based Indian Call Centre* – which was kind of self-explanatory. The show was at lunch time in Finnegan's Wake, a little Irish pub off Cowgate. The show went well by all accounts. It was free entry and was full every day – on some busier dates there was no standing room. This was the first time people had come specifically to see me perform and it was like nothing else, it filled me with gratitude.

My second stint at the festival, in 2014, was much bigger with my show called *I Am Not Malala*.* It was inspired by the fact that when I'd first heard Malala

---

* Malala Yousafzai is a Pakistani education activist and the youngest Nobel Laureate.

Yousafzai's story, my gut reaction had been, if there was a shooting at my school, I'd have stayed home. At the time of writing the show, I managed to get in touch with journalist Christina Lamb who co-wrote Malala's autobiography *I Am Malala* to help me curate my content. Christina shared some warm anecdotes about how Malala once asked why Bono wore 'shades indoors' and how she had received a bouquet from Angelina Jolie to her crib in Birmingham – standard. I was excited to share my comedy as I'd been working meticulously on the routine to ensure it was as funny as possible. I spent way more money as it was my second time up there and I was convinced it would be a stepping stone to making me a pro.

It was a disaster.

The venue, unbeknown to me, was miles from the centre, and the Jehovah's Witnesses, who I was flyering alongside, received more interest than me.

I'd heard of bad Edinburghs from other comedians on the circuit, and a part of me downplayed their experiences thinking they were being dramatic. That was until it happened to me. That's when I fully understood the nightmare. I ended up changing venues to another one mid-fringe, a room on the Royal Mile, but the timing was atrocious – it was at 11.15 a.m. I could, in theory, perform a show at the Fringe any time I wanted. But I was now invisible because my venue change wouldn't be corrected in the Fringe guide (this was before apps). I went to the Fringe office where other comedians were sticking five-star reviews on to the posters. With no reviews myself, I manually changed venue information on my circa 5,000 flyers and amended the 100 posters I had managed to place non-strategically around various venues (many of them buried underneath the other show posters plastered over them) and carried on.

I flyered every day for at least an hour and a half before the show, and though more and more people came, it wasn't anywhere near as good as the London previews, which rendered it a flop. It was definitely a learning curve. One of the things that stayed with me was it wasn't the number of people who came to see me, what mattered was that the ones who came had a genuine interest in my show.

I didn't know if I could come back from this but I clung on to my dignity and pushed forward, leaving the rain, disappointment and Irn-Bru behind.

A few months after Edinburgh, I mentioned to Christina that I would be performing a live show for the BBC Asian Network* that was being recorded in

---

* A network that primarily caters to Asian audiences, which many comedians have mixed feelings about. On the one hand it gives coverage, on the other, it sometimes feels like we're being typecast by the BBC.

Birmingham, where Malala lived, and she said she'd check if Malala could come along.

The day of the gig I went to my local beauty salon and it was my beautician Nafisa's last day. She had to go back to India for an 'emergency'.* She did my make-up and unfortunately made me look really white, but by the time she handed me a mirror to see the results I didn't have time to ask for any changes, I had a train to catch.† I put on a pink reptile satin suit and took the train from Euston station to Birmingham, hoping people wouldn't take too much notice of my now varied skin tone. On arrival, I met the other comedians on the bill, all male. And their entourages. It's funny how male comedians always travelled with an entourage whereas I was always on my own.

It turned out Malala‡ had a rare window in her busy schedule and had graciously accepted the invite. I was thrilled that I would meet her. There were few Asian women from my culture who have been such a huge inspiration, and this was such a big deal given her humanitarian efforts and busy life. When Malala walked

---

* To non-Asians, an Indian emergency could be eloping, a family member dying or a VISA/right to remain being revoked, causing immigration difficulties.

† Asian make-up artists tried to lighten my skin and white make-up artists tried to darken my skin colour. They were both strange experiences as they were at least two shades off my actual skin colour.

‡ Even Malala is married now!

into the room, it buzzed with energy. I was completely humbled by how generous she was with her time and spirit and I loved how she was both gracious and elegant. It was just so lovely to meet her, and I thanked her emphatically for coming. To me, Malala represents strength and overcoming adversity.

That evening she was wearing a traditional salwar kameez with a matching brown scarf covering her head. She said I could touch her head and that some people didn't believe that she had brain surgery. She also told me about the difficult ordeal she had been through. It had only been two years since she'd left Pakistan at that point. I assured her that I believed her and it wasn't necessary. Malala was everything I had expected her to be and more. I was so impressed by her bravery and her dedication to girls' education, it made me happy that young Asian girls would have such an iconic role model to look up to. Talking to her it was like I knew her; she was incredibly humble and great company. Though I loved talking to her, I didn't want to take up too much of her time as I was wary of how highly sought after she was. When we stopped chatting, we just sat comfortably and watched her brother playing and running around in the room. She smiled at him, clearly amused. I checked if she wanted anything to eat or drink, which is one of my strongest Asian traits, and soon she was ushered off by one of the production team to sit in the audience.

I was really looking forward to the show although I was a little nervous and not just because it was being recorded, but Malala would be watching me make jokes associated with her. I hoped she and the whole crowd would like the routine and the way I was taking a stand about the fact that an ethnic woman's presence was *always* rooted in her trauma, or the trauma of the wider ethnic group. It was so fucked up the way people, mostly white, fawned over a pre-adolescent and delighted over something that would have been incredibly challenging and painful for Malala – being shot and leaving her place of birth. American musician Billy Joel's statement, around the time she was receiving brain surgery, that hearing about Malala getting shot 'cured his depression' was yet another example of the perverse ways in which Asians were seen and that our conditions, no matter how dire, were infantilised and used as a springboard for other people's morale.

I was beside myself with happiness that I was able to make her laugh that day – my sister is a real one!

Last year Canada granted Malala honorary citizenship.

Like it's not tough enough being Pakistani and British, now she's got to be Canadian enough too!

Couldn't they have at least waited until her 18th birthday before giving her a third nationality?

Then Billy Joel came out and said that,
'Hearing about Malala getting shot cured my depression.'

Well that sure is a relief, as long as it bucked up the guy who wrote 'Uptown Girl'.

Do you think he's heard about the missing schoolgirls?

Cos if hearing about Malala getting shot cured his depression then hearing about over two hundred missing Nigerian schoolgirls is really going to bring back his funk.

He's not going to be depressed for a while!

Career flops:

♡ Not getting into the Pleasance Reserve two years in a row. This is a comedy showcase that takes place every year at one of the 'Big Four'

Edinburgh venues. In their response, they told me they *loved me*, but it was a no.

♡ Not getting a TV producer* to sleep with me (not for a job).

♡ Not getting on to any BAME scheme.

♡ Not getting on TV because my material was racy. Apparently adult audiences need to be protected from sexual innuendo, which is funny in a world where *Naked Attraction* exists.

♡ Being kicked off the Muslim circuit which at the time consisted of like four Muslim acts. This is a lot more than there used to be.

♡ Not getting the part as the pretty wife in the movie *Victoria and Abdul*. They asked me to speak in Urdu at the audition and at best I speak broken Urdu.

♡ Not getting the part as the matchmaker in *What Is Love* – I just didn't hear back.

♡ Not getting to write an essay for *It's Not About the Burqa*.

♡ Not getting any articles published in mainstream papers.

♡ Being hired as the token Asian by BBC Studios comedy to tick a box.

♡ Being released by BBC Studios comedy once said box was ticked.

---

* Hi, if you're reading this, and no, I'm no longer interested.

♡ Having my episode of Off Menu podcast cancelled. Maybe for role-playing sex.

The comedy commissioner for Radio 4 had come to the *I Am Not Malala* show. I remember following up with her in December after the Fringe that year and pitching a Radio 4 show to her. Apparently, everyone who is anyone got where they are because of their Radio 4 show. She said that she had been surprised to see me bring my show to the Fringe, as she had thought I should have taken a bit more time to prepare my debut. After a long meeting, where I had tried my hardest to impress her with my ideas, she finished by saying that she was no longer going to be the commissioner and that it was nice meeting me anyway. Without a Radio 4 show, which I'd understood was the next step towards success post-Edinburgh, it felt like I'd wasted eight grand putting on a forgettable show. There'd been such hype to live up to for my 'first' show that it had distracted me from the show I was making. I didn't know what to do next. At nearly twenty-five I was lost, neither progressing in my comedy, banking career or personally in my love life.

I think when you are in your twenties, you are supposed to have your whole life together and any side hustles should have the potential to become full-time careers. It's this pressure along with the feeling that our work should be intrinsically linked with our purpose that I think leaves so many of us feeling unfulfilled, like we are losing all the time. But the reality is, life is an ongoing process and journey, there is no final point at which you find happiness, society massively underrates contentment. So, I think it's important to show you some of the ups and downs in my comedy experience because one thing is for sure, it isn't always a laugh! Most of the time it's hard to even feel like a comedian at all, particularly when all the acts that I saw who progressed, didn't look or sound anything like me. I would do appearances and interviews, but it felt like something was missing. I felt I needed to prove something to myself, but I didn't know what or how.

During this time I'd go to small gigs at London pubs and was preoccupied. I had to force myself to smile when usually I was bubbly. The comedians would talk among themselves and crack jokes and be enjoying the moment and I didn't feel anything. I didn't want to be a part of it. I felt like I had tried so hard at it and I just didn't want to fight any more to get the opportunities that most acts got easily. I cared too much, which meant I couldn't let go and I felt like a phony for not enjoying it. I didn't really consider myself a comedian at all at this point. I might have been recognised at events now and again by the general public but I wasn't a regular on the telly. To be a comedian did you have to be someone who knew everyone or someone everyone knew?* It was such a strange time for me, to be both regularly featured in the country's newspapers, in interviews and Fringe press features, but still not have any credibility within my industry. I love comedy, but it didn't feel like it loved me.

I couldn't really admit my doubts to anyone. Comics would just tell me I was being silly, start spreading rumours of a meltdown or mistake it for either publicity or being a typical comedian who needed their ego stroked. My friends didn't understand either and constantly asked, 'When are you going to be on telly?' As if it was as simple as that. They didn't understand everything that went on behind the scenes to get to that point. The hustle of getting stage time, performing to small rooms, failing, getting back up, being lost, refining material, writing on the back of my hand and jotting down Post-it notes and iPhone notes at 4 in the morning. They were attracted to the glamour of it and nothing else. It's the same with all celebrity, it's a dream until you're in it; grafting, working, hoping, worrying and just trying to keep your head above water.

I felt low and I retreated from the world. I lost my

---

* I've since learnt the true mark of being a comedian is no longer getting calls/texts from close ones asking why I'm 'like that' or checking whether I'm OK as they've learnt to normalise my state of disarray.

nerve and had a terrible case of writer's block. For the first time in my life, I started questioning whether I was funny.

I came home from that Edinburgh to find a big white parcel waiting for me. I didn't recognise the sender. I opened it to find the cuddly toy and fan mail I had given to the lady to pass on to Chris Rock. I noticed a tiny scribble on the envelope, 'Sorry, Chris Rock's management refuses to accept any items from fans. Hammersmith Apollo'. I threw the fan mail and cuddly toy in the bin. Waster !

13

Suicide Squad

Comedy was the least of my worries. In the beginning my father's affair had started with the best of intentions. He wanted to preserve his first family's sanctity while also protecting the other woman's reputation from a community in India that would quickly write her off for not keeping her own marriage. My father would split his time between the two households, alternating three to four nights at each place every other week. This went on for a long while until he started to favour the other family over us. At that point he'd spend a measly one or two nights with my mum and the rest of the time at the other woman's. Towards the end, his intentions had clearly given way to his passions, and he'd literally drop by to see my mum for an hour a day, maintain his handle on the situation, and spend seven nights with the other woman.

The affair had morphed into an endeavour to keep questions from his first family at bay. A few years and an illegitimate baby later, on a trip to India, he secretly married the other woman. It was only at this point that my mum became aware that this woman would be more than a little side pussy, and that she wasn't going anywhere.

In India, it isn't uncommon for men to have multiple wives, and though Mum was crushed, I think she tried to normalise the situation in her head. Because of this she selflessly supported the second wife through each of her pregnancies. My mum not only helped her deliver the children but also helped raise them with no thanks or real understanding from my dad or the other woman. My mum didn't realise that she had Stockholm syndrome,* that she'd been conditioned to accept this situation and the way my dad behaved as normal. Like I said earlier, it is common for women to have very low marital expectations, and so my mum continued to give and give in the hope of some love in return. Her self-worth was in shreds.

My father in the beginning had been very happy with my mother. He'd come to England because of

---

* A psychological response where abuse victims develop a bond with the ones hurting them.

her. He used to cook and work and he supported her with little complaint. He was content until the second wife convinced him he wasn't. Eventually, the sharing stopped and I felt the second wife had grown emboldened and greedy. After twenty years it seemed that she had outgrown her position as the second wife. She wanted to be the only wife. It appeared that she would do anything to gain that honour.

My mother and I knew this was going on but had no way of stopping it. My mum put on a brave face for so long. We also didn't appreciate our right to walk away from it. My father continued to play happy families with us, spending increasing amounts of time with his other family, as if the situation was totally normal. We became weakened through suppressing our own pain and she became stronger and more confident in wielding her power over us. She invited my mum into her home and openly canoodled with my father in front of her, whereas my parents remained physically separate. My mum told me how small it made her feel years later, but only when it was too late.

Looking back with the benefit of hindsight, it's clear how wrong and manipulative this all was, but at the time I was so oblivious to it because I blindly attached trust to my father. I would never in a million years have believed he would be capable of hurting me. But honestly, what he did makes the dads who pop out for milk and never come back look like 'saints' – at least they don't parade their affairs and new family in front of their old family and community. My mum and the whole family were trained to protect my father – the official line was that he was 'carrying the burden of two families' – as opposed to the truth, which was, he was just looking out for himself and wanting his cake and eating it. And I always worried that he would end up in trouble if the police found out he had two wives, which was illegal in the UK. I didn't realise, growing up, that the second Islamic marriage wasn't even recognised in this country.

The lies, the manipulation and exploitation were all too much for my mother. They culminated in Mum attempting suicide by taking a number of pills. This wasn't long after I'd taken her out for dinner to celebrate her birthday. After being kept in hospital under observation for a few hours, she was discharged.

I had been at work all day and didn't really see the extent of it all. When I tried to talk to her about it, Mum was too drained from the ordeal and just spent a few days trying to sleep it off. I felt so guilty. I wondered what I could have done differently. I was in a state of shock and instead of taking time to understand what had happened, I tried to keep things moving.

Two months later my mum made a second attempt and this time she tried a higher number of pills. Dad was indifferent, he kept up his daily visits to the home for about an hour, before going to the other woman. I was terrified that she might do it again, and I made her promise she wouldn't. I would plead with her to come to me if she had suicidal thoughts or feelings again. My college psychology teacher, who lost a friend to suicide, said that people who are suicidal often never tell anyone. But I failed to see this and continued applying rationale to an irrational situation. I tried being more attentive. I moved her into a room with more natural light, saw to it she had enough money and the food she wanted. But when someone is mentally unwell and has had such harm inflicted on them over twenty years, essentially, getting better just doesn't seem like it's on the cards. As we found out.

The third time she attempted suicide with pills, she took a lot more, and was in a near-fatal condition and was admitted into intensive care.

When my mum was discharged from intensive care, during the senior psychologist's assessment, he asked her what had brought about these incidents. My mum simply replied, 'I'm old, my kids are grown up and I've got nothing to live for.' She was defeated and, beyond marriage, she felt there was nothing else for her in the world. There were no new chapters without her husband, who was everything to her.

Ultimately, I think my mum had felt victimised and didn't know where to turn. Having lost her mother to suicide at a young age, and with her father no longer with us, she craved the stability that a family with a mother and father would provide. She wanted what my father stood for so much that she was willing to totally overlook how he treated her and the pain he caused her. She didn't feel like she could divorce him, partly due to the pressure within her community and culture, but also because she couldn't fathom what leaving him and being independent would mean. The matrimonial vows are so final – '*till death do us part*' is pretty strong wording – and often it's hard to walk away from this. It implies that it's your duty to put up with anything and everything in a marriage. I reckon vows could do with some caveats such as '*but if you dare to cheat or do me wrong then you can get to fuck!*'

My mum had mental health problems from the age of nineteen, and her mother before her, so as a community we are not immune. Sadly, Asian society is often painstakingly brutal and unforgiving, particularly to older women. After they have completed their work as the housekeeper, mother and carer for their children, they tend to be written off.

The reason I wanted to share this story, painful though it is, is to shed a light on mental health problems among the Asian community. In one UK study, middle-aged Pakistani men and older Indian and Pakistani women reported significantly higher rates of depression and anxiety compared to similarly aged white people, even after taking into account differences in socio-economic status. Other studies have demonstrated particularly high susceptibility among South Asian immigrant females to self-harm and certain mental illnesses, including depression, anxiety, insomnia and eating-related psychopathology.* Part of the reason for this, according to Professor Dinesh Bhugra, an expert in mental health at King's College London, is that the South Asian population has 'a bigger notion of shame' than others in the UK. Many also fear that acknowledging mental illness might prevent them from getting married – and as we have seen marriage is a huge concern in my community. Dr Bhugra says he has found that many in the community do not consider mental illness a medical issue, but instead put it down to other factors such as a 'superstitious belief' that it's caused by something they did in a previous life and so they're being 'punished'.†

From these experiences with my family and seeing what my mum went through I learnt from an early age how self-serving people could be and, being a minor, normalised it. Though I realised the importance of

---

* Alison Karasz, et al. 'Mental Health and Stress Among South Asians.' *Journal of Immigrant and Minority Health*, vol. 21, Supplement 1 (2019): 7–14.

† 'Why Do South Asians View Mental Illness as Taboo', 4 September 2016. See https://www.bbc.co.uk/news/uk-england-36489893

having agency over my own life and decisions very early on, it still requires a conscious effort for me to put it into practice. While I believed (and still do believe) that love is one of life's best pleasures, I didn't want to get to the point, like my mum, where it defined me or that I was solely reliant on a partner in any way. I overcompensated with Ray J, having such little expectations of him, and neglected myself in doing so.

I realised during this time that abuse isn't only the harmful things someone does to their partner, but also the things they don't do. Being neglectful, distant and always receiving and never giving can be abusive too. Though I do believe there is usually one person in a relationship that loves that bit more, for love to work it should be as balanced as possible between giving and receiving. A partner is meant to give you life, not squeeze it out of you. I wish I had realised that if someone keeps on taking, without giving back, it leaves you at a loss, mentally, physically and even materially. There's only so long one person can be strong for, and the best relationships are when partners are in sync or can at least talk about it when they're not. With any partner, you need to know them inside and out and understand any sickness or ailment* they may have or develop, so you know the best way to help them, and also how it may impact you.

I've always been a giving person but proving and

---

* Could be spiritual not just a physical illness.

showing my love has to be within reason, and something I want to do. If it isn't being reciprocated, then I need to ask myself the tough question: why am I with someone who doesn't make me happy?

In the words of late, great comedian Patrice O'Neal:

'I can only love somebody 90 per cent, that's the most love I can give and that's the highest. Because I have to save 10 per cent to survive in case that person ain't shit. In case they leave me, in case they cheat. If you go 100 per cent, what have you got left for you?'*

Ultimately, I've come to realise that women should feel empowered to choose a path that suits us, even if tradition says it should be otherwise. A break up is better than a breakdown. Even though people may have complained that I don't exemplify a traditional Asian woman, it doesn't mean I don't appreciate my culture or my Asian heritage. I will always urge women to care for themselves rather than to entirely forsake themselves for others. Our mental health is too important.

Growing up in such a pressure-cooker household did not equip me with the best skills to form lasting and effective relationships. It made me scared to trust, even though I hungered for that connection that was promised to me in all of the TV programmes and films

---

* From *Opie and Anthony* with Patrice O'Neal radio show.

I watched growing up, and the music I listened to. Finding a relationship seemed like a huge risk, and I didn't want to be in a position where someone could potentially break my spirit.

Maybe if we revered a woman's spirit in the same way we do her virginity, the world would be a completely different place.

Things that help my mental health:

- ♡ Hearty food – see heart health foods specifically
- ♡ Love
- ♡ Music
- ♡ Acupuncture
- ♡ Exercise/Movement
- ♡ Friends
- ♡ Sleep
- ♡ Ayurvedic herbal teas*/warm water throughout the day
- ♡ Journalling, especially looping thoughts
- ♡ Talking to trusted professionals. Please don't solely rely on YouTube videos or Google as a source for medical advice.

---

* Ayurveda is the world's oldest healing holistic system. There are different dietary recommendations to suit the different dosha types (Vata, Pitta and Kapha).

- ♡ Using a foot massager (optional additions epsom salts or lavender oil) to raise vibrational frequency.
- ♡ Going easy on the dairy (trust me, I've done the research).
- ♡ Sauna

Things that help me sleep (sleep is so important to recover and recharge your mind, which is why it gets its own section):

- ♡ Prayers
- ♡ Indian Gooseberry/Amla is really high in vitamin C. When vitamin C-rich fresh fruit is out of season I use amla powder.
- ♡ Smells, particularly lavender and jasmine candles. If I'm really struggling, I use essential oils on my pressure points like temples/wrists.
- ♡ Sex. Important to say that this is *before* not during!
- ♡ Ashwagandha* Turmeric Moon Milk
- ♡ Massage
- ♡ Nature sounds (especially rain) and calming podcasts

---

* NB ashwagandha is an aphrodisiac – as I found out myself not so long ago!

14

Crazy, Stupid Love

It had been three years since I'd known Ray J, I was twenty-seven years old and I still hadn't had sex with him. I was doing something incredibly destructive in trying to barter sex with me for commitment, but I couldn't stop myself continuing down this path. I didn't realise that if a man wants to stay he will, regardless of what I did for him sexually and romantically. But with Ray J I genuinely thought sex might save our relationship and make him stick around for good. It might even make him love me.

Then one day, I decided to make it happen. I was going to get my back blown out. I booked an Ibis hotel in Essex on a Thursday night in autumn. I got there early, showered, dried my hair and left it down.

I did full make-up and wore a banging black dress. He texted:

What room?

I texted him the floor and room number and opened the door for him as seductively as I could. Before this moment we'd tried to have sex a fair few times, but it hadn't happened for one reason or another. This day though, there was something in the air that meant we both knew it was going to happen. We didn't say much beforehand.

He wore a crisp, white shirt that made him look so much sexier than normal. He came in and sat on the bed and I gravitated towards him as he started to unbutton his shirt cufflinks first. When we kissed I felt what I'd been looking for from him all along – that he wanted me. All of me.

It didn't last long. We didn't talk afterwards and both fell asleep. The sex and wanting had passed and it was incredibly . . . anticlimactic. It was a great preview into what intimacy could be. I had hoped it would feel like the Niagara Falls were gushing out of me but the reality was more of a half-orgasm. Which is exactly what it sounds like – kind of like eating a burger without the bun (or any sauce or cheese) – or like getting to the best part of your favourite song and your AirPods running out charge. I didn't realise that for it to have been what I wanted I would have needed more from him. He should have made more of an effort rather than just showing up. Mind you, even if he did, and I communicated what I liked, who knows if I'd have got there. The female orgasm is a cruel mistress. Anyway, the fact is it didn't change anything between us because what I didn't realise at the time was there was no us.

Post-nut clarity had us feeling even more distant than before and I felt as if I could barely reach him in that relatively small double bed. So after a restless night, I left him sleeping as I had to head to work. The change I thought would come with no longer being a virgin was absent. It didn't change me into a sexy siren or a loved woman. I was a virgin for so long and now I just wasn't one, end of story. I couldn't kiss it goodbye; it was gone. It was too embarrassing to share with anyone at my age and I also didn't think I wanted to hear the truth people would dish out to me about Ray J. It left me wide open and more alone than before. As a virgin I knew who I was and now I didn't have a clue.

I was, however, incredibly horny and, after that first time, I waited for the sex to continue to be the satisfying and thrilling wild ride I'd long been promised. But the sex was all about Ray J. I entrusted myself to him entirely, and in that trust, I thought he'd care about my experience and my enjoyment. He was my first everything – kiss, touch, fuck – but you'd have thought it was the other way around in the lack of knowledge he had in pleasing me.

It was good or at least it was fine for me, but each time I knew something was missing. Sometimes he'd quip, 'I got mine, it's up to you to get yours.' I wish I was joking.

If you are a woman reading this, you will not be surprised by the following sentence – I never had a single orgasm with Ray J. I didn't blame him at first, I just thought I couldn't orgasm because we lacked an emotional connection. (Once he even had the audacity to complain that I didn't orgasm, despite doing nothing to help make it happen.) The sex was rough and raw and new but there was no intimacy, romance or long-drawn-out passionate moments. He refused to use condoms as he said he couldn't abide them or that he was 'allergic' to them, and I didn't want to use birth control because of the side effects. He assured me he was 'safe', that he would always pull out. And I believed him.

Men will really say anything to get their way. Ray J was happy and satisfied he'd got what he wanted. As for me, I was left hoping he would transform into the partner I was craving – one that truly valued me. He never did.

Things I wish I'd known before losing my virginity:

- ♡ It won't make him love you.
- ♡ It will probably make you want more sex.
- ♡ It doesn't hurt for everyone.

♡ You probably won't orgasm your first time.

♡ You probably won't orgasm a lot of times after that as well.

♡ If you want a man to use a condom, he should, otherwise don't have sex with him.

♡ Let the guy pay for dinner, it's the least he can do.

♡ Intimacy and care are more important than sexy and rough.

Not only was the sex unreciprocated, I was also doing the lion's share in arranging and paying for dates. I would pay for hotels for him to come and fuck me in. Sometimes he would stay but most of the time he would leave straight afterwards. It was not a good feeling to be left alone after having sex, and to have everything on his terms. One time I booked a swanky hotel, the New Providence Wharf, in the hopes of creating some romantic moments for us. Ray J, walking like he owned the place but also like it was totally beneath him, looked at the wall art and sniggered, 'That's hideous.' We had obligatory sex and then watched *Limitless* in HD in silence.

Ray J had a habit of undermining me. He knew I was dabbling in comedy and one time after sex he blurted out, 'Women aren't funny. Women can't be funny, but I'd fuck a comedian.' I shrugged it off despite it being such a personal and specific dig at me and the life I was trying to create. It made me reluctant to share this aspect of my life with him, particularly as he himself was a closed book. The most he ever shared was that he was 'horny and tired, in that order'.

The thing is there's puppy love and there's the way I loved Ray J. I was so far gone that although his ways would hurt at times, I always brushed it off. This is something I think all women can relate to, when you are with a guy and you *really* like him, if not love him, it's so hard to see the red flags and the warning signs. You make excuse after excuse for him and pray for a change that will likely never come. It takes an incredibly self-assured woman to see negative behaviour and walk away when she's deep in her feelings for him.

Ray J didn't like any of the 'soft' stuff. He wouldn't cuddle. He didn't compliment. He certainly would never hold my hand. He didn't even let us have a photo together. That's got to be a measure of a relationship right? Things he didn't want to do included talking about his feelings and so I kept mine bottled up as I knew he wouldn't listen. It got to a point where I developed a taste for, and even an addiction to the pain. I think this was a way of controlling me, as when he would hurt me, I became dependent on him to ease the pain I felt instead of acknowledging the problem myself and escaping the relationship. I denied that I was in pain and, like my mum, in the early stages of developing Stockholm syndrome myself.

It's sad to think I was relying on and caring for the one person who hurt me the most. He refused to lay his cards on the table at any point. I once asked if he even liked me* and he said, 'I wouldn't be sleeping with you if I didn't.' Even though in the same breath earlier that day he'd said, 'Men will fuck anything that moves.' The worst part was that he always spoke about me to me. He would not address me directly but say, 'When you settle down with someone' and completely deny that we were an item. As well as denying me, he also denied my identity. Ray J was an atheist and as such had a disdain for Islam. He didn't like the faith. I sometimes wondered if he treated me the way he did due to his poor perception of Muslims.

I didn't know how to stand up for myself and my needs for fear of losing him. He had always been upfront that he wasn't looking for anything long term and so I thought I was the one who was being too demanding or misreading things. I just never believed in myself. There were times I'd grow tired of our 'arrangement' and complain, but every single time I brought it up it fell on deaf ears.

'You're ruining it,' he'd reply. 'It's best when things are kept simple. We meet up, have a good time. Just accept it for what it is. I don't have anything more to give.'

---

* If you have to ask your partner repeatedly if they love you, chances are they don't.

I didn't want to play games as I didn't believe it was right. But the reality is, by not playing the game, I played myself and lost. There isn't a ceremony or anything to be revered in my freedom or autonomy in running my affairs. Quite the contrary, society (non-Muslims and Muslims alike) saw me as astray, or odd for not having settled down. I had been against arranged marriages on principle because I struggled to see the difference between that and pimping. I thought a woman deserved so much more than to be traded on a free market. But then I allowed myself to be sold short. There's an irony in the fact that I took such pride in dodging an arranged marriage only to end up in the messiest of arrangements on far less favourable terms. No dowry, no flowers, no respect. Instead of wedding plans, or plans for the future, Ray J's plans were when, where and how high he could push my legs up while he was shagging me.

In a shocking moment, Ray J asked me what turned me on and I was excited to suggest some things that might lead to a happy ending for me. And so I told him I really had a thing for doing it outdoors. Listen, we all have our kinks, OK? I even suggested the toilet at our local Nando's. What can I say, I don't go clubbing and it was the best I could come up with on a budget! I would really have preferred it on board an airplane but with the heat Muslims already get on flights, that wasn't going to happen. Anyway, he just wouldn't agree with going outdoors and so we carried on the same standard fucking. Same positions, same duration, same sex talk. It was such a disappointment.

First, don't ask what your partner wants and then not oblige!

Second, it affirmed to me that he was making sure his needs were met irrespective of whether mine were or not.

I even tried with less riskier propositions, for instance playing with food in the bedroom. That was also met with disapproval. 'I don't mix food and sex.' Like not even whipped cream?

I asked if he'd finish in my mouth, he said no. I mean, what more could he want from a girl?

Fucking him felt regimented.* He liked what he liked and that was the end of it. I mean, it's great when guys can be dignified and gentlemanly, but it was as though he was trying to push me into a box, or even discipline me.

Sex was meant to be about letting go, exploring new heights with one another, but rather than collaborating, we were going to play to his tune and his tune alone. I know now it's rare for guys to stop during sex to make it more enjoyable for their partner, even if they sense they're not experiencing maximum pleasure. I haven't met a single man who didn't put his sexual pleasure first and foremost. I'm not sure I would know how to

---

* He wouldn't take his top off during sex :(

consort with a man who didn't (actually I'd never let him out of my sight), but the point is, I also should have taken responsibility for my own satisfaction. I didn't want to confront what was staring me in the face: if he wasn't willing to negotiate, then no matter how much I liked him, I was only prolonging my own agony.

My head and pussy are intrinsically connected. If a guy has my mind, then he has my body. But that means I get fucked twice: first a head fuck then the actual sex. This is the biggest deterrent for me against casual sex. I didn't want my head messed with particularly as I feared mental health issues may run in my family and I didn't know what the consequences of this could lead to for me. This also made me confused as to why I liked guys. Was it the attention they gave me and the way they made me feel, even if it was bad most of the time? Whenever I think back to the minutes, seconds, hours I spent on Ray J, all I am left reminded of is being alone in the company of someone I had poured my heart and soul out to for nothing in return.

I'll never forget what Ray J once told me. And I quote, 'Everyone will let you down, it's being with someone who's worth being let down for.'

What about a relationship where no one lets you down?

Clearly that was not an option. It was his way of indicating I should keep my expectations low as the worst was yet to come.

15

Waiting to Exhale

I met my closest friend Monty at the posh bank call centre. She is the most loving and kindest person I know. She's a beautiful Nigerian woman, full-figured, with natural Afro hair, tall and always with a smile on her face. Confident and sassy, her laugh is the most soothing sound that would ease away all my worries time and again. The call centre was notorious for being anti-social as we had to stay strapped to our headsets, but someone had mentioned in passing to me that Monty was on the comedy circuit and as soon as we met, we hit it off. It felt like I'd known her for years. She was naturally funny and so real and understanding. She made me want to come out of the shell I'd hidden myself inside for years.

Monty is one of the rare people in my life who

accepted me for who I am and deeply cared for me. She also taught me how to cook rice, which is an essential skill I probably should have mastered by that point. We were a part of a small group of people from different ethnic backgrounds who worked at the institution and we bonded over our similar experiences. We both sounded English – Monty has the poshest accent I've ever heard – and were articulate, which could both be a gift and a curse. A gift in that it helped us to communicate with the people who surrounded us, but a curse in that it prompted so many unnecessary comments about our identities and experiences. We also both have ethnic-sounding names, which apparently conflict with the accents we have, and this attracted even more unprovoked commentary, such as, 'God, I can't believe you're Indian, Sadia' or 'You don't sound Nigerian at all, Monty.' Once we gave our colleagues an inch, they wanted a mile. It was like opening a gateway into an exchange where these curious bystanders felt entitled to know every crumb of detail about our parents' ancestry, educational level and, for me, my marital status.

We managed to get each other through the long days and shared in the ups and downs that working in a call centre prompted (of which there are plenty). Monty is full of life advice – often in the form of voice notes (a method of communication which allows for way more extensive life support from friends throughout the day, which I'm eternally grateful for). Her presence is a blessing to everyone lucky enough to cross paths with her. Now, I had been single for most of my adult life, and I couldn't count Ray J, who was never willing to commit and had the emotional capacity of a sock. His idea of intimacy was trying to guess my bra size. He felt my boob and said, '36C?' I asked him how he knew and he humble bragged, 'I used to work in the lingerie section of M&S.' For so long I hadn't had a close friend to lament to or bounce my worries off of, I'd just kept them pent up inside. And Monty was never scared to dish out the truth.

One weekend I called her. I was barely seeing Ray J and the thoughts of dating again seemed like stepping into the pits of hell. I moaned, 'Why can't I get a man?'

I could hear Monty sigh at the other end of the phone. 'Well, you have to try, Sadia. Have you tried online dating?'

'No,' I said defensively, curled up in my bed, looking up blankly at the white ceiling. Online dating seemed like a scary prospect – it was hard enough guessing people's intentions in real life, now I'd have to try and work it out over a screen? No, thanks.

Monty audibly rolled her eyes. 'Why not? I know a few friends who've found partners and even got married on there.'

'Let's be honest, guys will see pictures of me and

either think I'm looking for a jihadi,* or hope that I can get them a British passport.' I was careful to deflect any suggestions she made out of the sheer terror of putting myself out there again. Being single had been my identity for so long and I had always been the girl that guys overlooked, so anything that sought to change that felt like a threat.

'Listen, I ain't trying to give no guy a passport, or support him,' Monty confirmed. We started giggling.

Monty was also single but seemed more confidently so. She didn't hunger for that connection like I did. She shared some of her horror stories on the dating scene that didn't fill me with much hope. She told me about going on dates with dudes who didn't want to pay for their own dinner – this is feminism gone too far. Then there was the guy who spat out his dinner at her in conversation and the guy who smelled like cat piss. It just sounded like a warzone, and not the dates from the movies with hot topless men.

Monty admitted, 'I honestly can't be arsed with dating, it's such a ball ache. Online dating is shit and there are mad people out there! Also I don't have a great deal of patience for knobheads.' At least she tried, I thought, as I rolled over on my bed and tried to think about the positives of being a heterosexual woman in this day and age.

---

* Let's face it, this has multiple definitions. In this context, I used it to mean a person involved in a jihad 'militant'.

Monty, ever the positive voice, continued, 'Well, that's not the only way, you could try speed dating?* I went with a friend a few weeks ago and it was pretty good.'

'No.' I moaned again. At this point I knew I was being irritating but I couldn't help myself. 'I don't want to go looking for a man, I want him to come to me.' Fucking Disney. Why did you have to make it look so easy?

'Sadia, does your comedy come to you or do you go out and get gigs?'

'I go out and get it. I'm emailing everyone – writers, promoters, producers,' I explained.

Monty chuckled knowingly. 'Right, well, then it's the same with dating. How do you expect to find someone if you're not going to do any of the work?'

I knew she was right. I just didn't know where to start. I worried about it being compulsive – that if I started, I wouldn't be able to stop until I had found someone. But I think it was more about not wanting to get it wrong, it seemed an impossible feat, rather than being worried about finding love. I didn't know what I wanted, and to embark on a search without this information felt unlike me, reckless. My whole life,

---

* A lot of intuitive dating is forbidden by Islam: speed dating, tarot card readings, horoscopes. I wasn't outgoing nor was I up for the remote dating either. I preferred the chemistry I would strike up in person rather than relying on a photo which didn't give the whole picture.

society had told me what my life path should be, but as it hadn't come to fruition, I was totally lost. What happened next? The unknown was scary.

Deep down, I knew Monty was right. I'd need to make the effort to get myself better at reaching out to people and to be vulnerable to find what I was truly looking for. But one of the problems was I didn't have any dating prowess. Ray J hadn't exactly given me good practice for what a healthy dating scenario might look like. Hard work and time were what counted to grow a relationship into something special, not one-word text messages and fleeting moments of passion. The hard work just felt unfair given everything I'd experienced in my life so far – can't help a girl for wanting an easy ride! All the messages about love made it seem magical, but they didn't point towards any of the real stuff, like compromise and patience, that went along with it. All I wanted was what I had seen: instant gratification and quick wins.

I stubbornly avoided online dating, and dating in general, as I didn't know where to start and wasn't sure that I could handle it along with everything else I was juggling with work and comedy. Better to focus on my career and have disappointing sex with Ray J, than put my heart on the line.

16

The Social Network

I had performed a few corporate gigs at the bank I worked for as a favour to colleagues for charity events. I wanted to continue doing these because I'd heard famous comedians got paid five figures for these appearances. In the comedy world, that is serious dollar! Then one time I saw a Muslim Professionals networking event advertised on a noticeboard at work. Although I made a point not to get involved in social events too often, I thought I would go along as a spectator, acting in 'official capacity' as a comedian. It seemed a good way of networking, particularly as the Muslim professional audience was one that I would have common ground with.

It was held on a weekday evening after work during

Ramadan. The event was at Iftar* in Canary Wharf. It was embarrassing to attend alone but, in usual form, I'd failed to lure an unsuspecting plus-one along, as most people opted to spend Ramadan with their families. It started late as initially the turnout was small and there was a sense that the organisers were trying to wait it out in case some people were on Asian time.† The venue was a long boardroom with white walls and sensible black chairs set out in uniform rows. At the end of the room was a table of refreshments which had water and appetisers. I felt obliged not to indulge, mainly because this left me open to explaining to others the reason I wasn't fasting and therefore explaining to people I'd never met before that I was on my period. Of course, other Muslims already knew this, but we would have still had that awkward exchange.

As the night had been billed a 'social event', I had had great expectations. I thought it would be lively and there would be banter and I'd meet fun, young Muslims who would tell me amazing stories. It sent a reeling reminder of how we tended to only socialise for and around charity nights. Either that or at weddings.

Luckily, I didn't struggle in striking up a conversation. As a comedian, I don't take myself very seriously

---

* Means 'break fast'. The meal served at the end of the day during Ramadan.

† Late.

at all which means I can usually chat freely to people. But that evening, everyone around me was trying to create a perfect impression and I couldn't figure out why. What did it matter? Over the evening, people kept telling me their qualifications and job titles. 'I've completed an MBA in Business,' one guy said. 'I'm a Chartered Accountant with ACCA,' a woman added. 'I'm a lawyer,' another man commented. 'I'm a major in Computer Science,' the next person revealed. It struck me that instead of the hijab, their identities were their qualifications; more often than not they didn't even mention their names. Given that I didn't have much insight into these professions, and felt wholly under-qualified in their company, I tried changing the topic to something more lighthearted until I was ushered into another group to do it all over again.

Even my half-hearted hopes to pull were a complete non-starter. The few men who were present were compelled to begin sentences with 'My wife's at home', 'I'm married' or 'I've got a family'. It seemed here the only thing that got these guys' attention was an act of charity. If there was a dam that needed building overseas, they came alive. Homeless kids in need of food and water and the men were ready for action.

It struck me that though this wonderfully talented and educated room full of people had spent all their lives labouring in pursuit of academic prestige and successful employment, they had done so at the cost of their social lives. They were all very well presented and nice but there was a feeling like we didn't know how to enjoy the fruits of all of that. It made me feel as though all British Asians were about was working and serious endeavours, and having fun was a distraction. Perhaps because this was the focus in our upbringing, and we had been taught to be reward-driven, we rarely explored beyond this. I was guilty of this myself: my reason for attending the event had been to network and get work. There was little connectivity between us, even though everyone outside the room felt as though we were somehow all identical. That room showed me how distant from each other we really were.

I didn't tend to let go and move without a care, as this often went hand in hand with drinking alcohol and that, obviously, I didn't participate in. It was the reason why it took me so long to find my voice in comedy, because that was all about letting go, being vulnerable and frankly being an idiot. It went against everything I knew. In this room, I saw that everyone else was similarly struggling to relax and let go, the exact opposite of the rooms I'd experienced in the comedy world.

While the Muslims at these networking events were socially crippled, but very successful and financially stable, the comedians I'd bump into were financially crippled and socially successful or eccentric depending on who it was. Our artistic and creative achievements were arguably rendered as unsuccessful, as soft things like 'finding your voice' and 'making a room full of people laugh' were all commendable but weren't an achievement until we were earning large sums of money. Quite frankly we were lucky to have our travel costs reimbursed.

It brought home that I was losing on both fronts. I wasn't earning the full financial potential that I'd most probably have reached if I'd pursued a traditional career path as an Asian, but equally I didn't have any of the social skills or pay-offs that made being in comedy a saving grace. I was gaslit by reality, too Asian for the comedy crowds and too much of a clown to be among all these high-flying Asians. Everyone around me looked and seemed so content that evening and I felt progressively more alone. Given that the event was a major snooze-fest, I consoled myself with the thought of dinner. Asian events were nothing without lots of food and I knew that I'd feel consoled by some grub. Well, at least I had thought I would. Turns out there was no food. This was put down to it being an event for charity. I was beside myself. Why call something an Iftar event and not have food? It was shocking.

I went home hungry and horny.

17

On the Basis of Sex

Reader, sadly I continued to have sex with Ray J, in fact I couldn't stop. I was living on my own and his visits were the only thing I could seek comfort in. We had waited so long and there was so much pent-up energy there. Thankfully it had gotten better, mainly because I had stopped focusing on trying to please him. The sex made me push our emotional incompatibility further to one side. It was the only thing we were semi-good at, but each and every time, rather than it bringing us closer together, it pushed him away. We would have sex and he would mumble goodbye or fall asleep. There was no goodbye kiss or hug – it was just cold.

It was a big deal to me, having pre-marital sex, as this wasn't something I had seen for myself. I was in denial about how none of this lived up to the hype. I should have been having the time of my life! Instead I became conditioned to the scraps Ray J offered me. I just thought that in relationships you had to take the rough with the smooth, and I kept hoping it would come good. I didn't want to give up on love as I hadn't planned for failure, but I didn't consider I could be waiting forever for things to change. At the same time, I couldn't accept that I was in a toxic relationship with myself, where more than anything I needed to love myself and see my value.

I wanted to know everything about him; past, present and future. I wanted to meet his friends and his family and be a part of his life, but he didn't listen. Even though I complained and got upset, it changed nothing. He had all of the power, leaving me to feel like I had to work hard to earn his attention, but having played the pussy card I was out of ideas. All I knew about getting a man was through using my body. I didn't know anything else. I wanted my pussy to mean more than a fling, but it was because he only saw my pussy and not my humanity that I was usable and disposable to him. I was convinced I'd held up my end of the bargain, so I was lost.

I remembered something from Chris Rock's set where he said, 'I've got to come back to commitment. And turn this old pussy into new pussy! That's right, I've got to recycle the pussy! I've got to recycle the pussy*! Because that's what a relationship is all about: recycling, keeping it new. If it ain't new, it's through!'† For this reason, I thought I should change tactics in order to 'keep it new', maybe I needed to be less desperate. Instead of being on call whenever he needed, I decided to be the exact opposite. I thought I should give him space and let him come to me. At my wits' end, I decided to stop texting him. I thought about him every day or occasionally every other day, but I thought maybe he needed time to miss me.

It was six months since I'd texted Ray J. No other prospects turned up, not that I was looking. He hadn't messaged me once in that time and although this told me everything I needed to know, I couldn't take no for an answer. I rewarded myself for my good behaviour by sending him a text. This was a few weeks after the Muslim Professionals event and, in fact, it may have been what prompted me to message. He replied asking to hook up. He didn't ask how I had been during the temporary ceasefire of texts, or why I'd suddenly got in touch. He knew he was the only one, which is why he was so entitled. I knew that wasn't the case where he was concerned. He never acted monogamously around me for a second.

I doubled down and said he'd have to do more than

---

* Women have to recycle the dick, if it ain't new it's through too!
† From Chris Rock, *Bring The Pain*, 1996

that. After having known each other for four years, I managed to coerce Ray J into taking me out on a date. He said he knew just the spot and I was excited. I knew I shouldn't have had to beg or wait so long, particularly as I had been giving him the goods. I chose a cute little number I'd got from ASOS, a black asymmetric skirt that I'd never worn before as I was saving it for the right occasion. I paired it with my favourite leopard print, organza transparent blouse with a black top underneath. I went to town on my make-up; as I concealed my hair, I always felt it a public duty to compensate with my face.

Ray J texted me he was outside, and I wondered where he had planned to take me. I thought about a plush restaurant he might have had lined up where there'd be waiters dressed in suits and we'd have to leave a healthy tip. Ray J enjoyed the finer things in life and since the build-up to our date had been a long time coming, and taken far longer than the time for us to have sex, I was hopeful that he was out to impress.

I got into the car and he started driving us through busy London streets – small talk was always kept to a minimum with us but our lack of conversation was just adding to my excitement and expectation. He stopped the car suddenly after ten minutes in East London and I thought maybe his car had failed or he needed to take a call.

'Get out,' he stated in his typically unenthusiastic style.

'Here?'

Not to be dramatic but we were in the ghetto.* Forest Gate, in a desolate street of empty, closed-down businesses, a place where weed was traded by day and cocaine by night. I couldn't hide my confusion.

'Yep, come on.'

He took me to a place called Yu Café. The shop looked like it was a fish market; the name was written in worn-out red lettering on a faded white background, cigarette stubs littered the floor outside and it was so run down it probably had been there since the Queen was born.

'Oh, forgot my beer.' He went to grab it from the boot. 'It's bring your own. You might want to think about losing that scarf, you know,' he commented nonchalantly as he fished around in his boot for a bottle.

I pretended to ignore this ridiculous statement.

We went into the small restaurant and there was no one inside. It was like one of those Chinese takeaways that never seemed to have any business but still

---

* The ghetto is a place that you have never seen if you're upper-/middle-class white people (unless of course you are scoping it out pre-gentrification). It's the equivalent of the 'projects' in the States. It's denoted by faeces and vomit on the streets. Stolen property being sold in broad daylight is the norm. Also denoted by broken shop windows, vandalism and fly-tipping.

operated nonetheless. The seating was white plastic picnic furniture. It was rough, and I noticed a health and safety warning notice. I wondered how they were even allowed to be open, then I saw a rat scurry past behind the kitchen that confirmed they most likely were not.

I was distraught, but Ray J didn't notice.

'I'll have the squid and rice,' he said to the guy serving at the counter before he came to take a seat – definitely no waiters in this place. This wasn't what I had expected at all. The meat wasn't halal* and I didn't want to go veggie. Actually I didn't want to eat there at all.

'Why did you bring us to this place?'

'It's just a place I come when I don't want to be seen,' he said casually as we sat down at one of the two tables. He deliberately chose the non-window table, not that there was a view. 'Look, are you gonna order?' His voice showed his irritation. The counter server was clearly impatiently waiting for my order. I felt rushed. When I asked to see a menu, they started speaking in a language I couldn't understand. 'Um, I'll have the prawns with rice,' I muttered defeatedly.

I couldn't hide my disappointment and barely touched my food. It was unlike me. I love eating and I'd saved all my daily calories to splurge on the date I thought we were going to have, but which he'd made crystal clear he didn't want us to be seen on.

---

* Meat permissible by Islamic law.

'Aren't you gonna have your prawns?' Ray J questioned while he polished off his beer. He'd already finished his meal.

'No.' My frustration was mounting by this point.

'Waste not want not. May I?' He was already reaching for my plate, pushing the food on to his own.

The person who had served us came over and asked if we wanted any coffee or desserts.

'No, thanks,' we both said in unison.

I paid for the meal as there was no offer from him to pay or even a move to get his wallet, put my coat on and headed back out to his car.

'Where we off to next?' Maybe he had something planned, a movie or some scenic sunset view.

Confusion passed over his face. 'Er, I've got to get away now.'

'But we're meant to be on a date, it's early. We've hardly got started!' I stumbled, shocked at the pathetic excuse of a date he'd put on for me.

'Yeah, but I've already spent time with you having dinner. I've got things to do.' He'd already made up his mind and he seemed inconvenienced by the conversation at this point. He was ready to get on his way.

It was so disheartening, being with someone, even for such a short space of time, who was obviously ashamed of me and had such rigid caveats on being seen together in public. I didn't know what Ray J's issue with me was – to be publicly associated with a woman, a woman in a headscarf (therefore the image of being with someone conservative) or whether it was something else that he felt would fracture his street cred. I guess a part of me had hoped that the date would change things, help me get under the surface of Ray J. I thought I could fix or change him the longer I persevered. Then I wondered if it was me. If there was something fundamentally wrong with me and that was why I didn't deserve love. Why it had to be such a battle for attention or reciprocity where I was concerned. Was I just supposed to be grateful for whatever I got?

In a state of mind that many women will understand, the thing I liked most about him was that I couldn't have him. In fact this meant I sort of worshipped him. He was of a higher class to me, from a middle-class family, and he'd often let me know it by talking down to me. He was so incredibly good-looking that I knew he was too good for me. But I couldn't find a way to let him go. I had learnt relationships were for keeps, for better or for worse, and that there was growth in the struggle. I had seen my own father give up on his marriage to my mother and I didn't want to fail by doing the same. I thought the harder I pushed and the more I struggled, I would get what I needed from him: love, respect and kindness.

Whenever I told anecdotes about Ray J to my friends, especially Monty, they were always unimpressed and advised caution. This only made me more determined to make the relationship work. In hindsight, I should have taken on the warnings from my friends and realised that if everyone had the same negative response to my partner then I should probably run the other way. I just didn't want to see. It showed my lack of self-worth as I considered Ray J and his treatment of me was all I deserved, and I think this is a feeling many Asian women go through. We are not conditioned to believe we are worthy of love. Instead we are told we are worthy of duty, hard work and silent resolve. Also as a Muslim woman, in the way I was brought up, my sexuality shouldn't have been my own. It belonged to men, so I misunderstood this fling as an equivalent of empowerment. But just because I was being liberal with my body, it didn't mean I was empowered. Far from it. Empowerment means to have and contain power, not someone having power over you. And this is why I know I cannot singularly blame Ray J. I should have believed in myself and my worth more.

Perhaps if bagging a man hadn't been so amplified in my culture, I could have had more perspective and made sure I hadn't put all my eggs in his basket. A part of me thought that being with him was better than being alone, or better than waiting for someone else and running the risk of going through the pain all over again.

I was wrong. Being with him, a man who far from

saving me was using me, I was more alone than without him. With him I didn't even have the chance to dream of a better future. The thing I wish I had known, before allowing myself to be entirely consumed by Ray J, or the idea of him, was the importance of starting as I mean to go on in a relationship. It's too easy to make compromises and sacrifices – particularly at the outset for the sake of the happiness of someone you're crazy about. But the beginning of a relationship truly should have been the happiest of times, and if I was entering into something dysfunctional, from the get-go, old habits die hard. If someone ritually takes advantage of their partner, it says a lot about who they are, and the longer you leave it the more embedded it becomes into the foundations of a relationship. It's not to say that at some point things wouldn't change, but it would be hard pushed given I had compromised myself and my feelings so much from the outset.

When someone's love so obviously wasn't forthcoming, should I have kept on trying? Perhaps, in retrospect, it wasn't wrong to have tried, but I should have set limits that protected myself and my own happiness.

How to spot a dickhead:

- ♡ People who always speak for you, without asking permission.
- ♡ Someone who says they want to tell you something and then says 'oh, it's nothing'.
- ♡ Users who always take and never give.
- ♡ Someone who feels their voice is louder and more important than others.
- ♡ Leaving someone unread and not replying straight away, or playing games.
- ♡ People who walk in front of you and stop in the middle of the pavement for no reason.
- ♡ A non-apology – 'I'm sorry *if* you've taken that the wrong way.' The most genuine apology is 'You made me see differently, I apologise.'*
- ♡ Anyone into the film noir genre.

---

* From Patrice O'Neal on *Opie and Anthony*.

18

Pride and Prejudice

Like my love life, my career wasn't going to plan. After my Edinburgh show flopped, I had taken time off the circuit to write a sitcom pilot. This had been all-encompassing, particularly the research. I worked on the project for eighteen months, chasing story leads and interviewing eighty people at my own cost. I developed the treatment, pilot and series format with help from an LA script editor I hired. Though it drew interest from several well-known production companies and several channels, and despite a promising pitch to Channel 4, it got turned down at the final round. Another project covering the theme, by an established writer, was commissioned instead. The response didn't console me either, 'The project was ahead of its time, which was ironic, given the story was based on true life events that were happening at the time. I knew what they meant. They wanted tried and tested, standard and boring. I knew this was the nature of my industry. They gave you hope, and you grafted away for little return. It didn't change my feelings of dejection. All that time and work. Although I knew it wasn't for nothing, I had learnt so much from the process, it felt like I hadn't achieved anything and that I had to pick up comedy where I had left it eighteen months ago, back at square one.

Since I hadn't performed comedy during this time – I'd favoured screenwriting over stand-up – I'd built up a fear of performing and got totally in my head about it. I hated being paralysed by fear. I knew I wanted to perform but I felt like I had lost my mojo. It shouldn't have been harder than when I started and that baffled me. I decided to see Lucy after a gap of nearly two years to try and get back on track. Talking through my ideas to generate material always helped me form routines in the past and I would sporadically connect with Lucy to do just that. I reflected back on the meetings I'd had with her and remembered how we didn't always find the same things funny. The odd times I tried to reference Chris Rock, she didn't approve. I had an idea criticising authority, for instance, and made a comparison to one of his routines, but she was quick to correct me, 'You don't have the following of a big, Black audience'. It left me feeling like she didn't understand where I was coming from. As time passed, I felt her increasingly 'Brownsplain'*, as though she had licence to speak on behalf of me and my experience just because she was in my vicinity. But I didn't voice my concerns, as a part of me felt that trying to change her would be mirroring the way she tried to change me. I wanted to try and be understanding over being right.

I felt that I often let her win arguments, as she tended to assert she was right and explain why. It seemed to me that these exchanges would end with her expecting an apology from me, even though I hadn't done anything other than be me. Comedy is subjective and I always felt like she didn't have to be there doing what she was for me so I let the little things slide. No one else was giving me their time like her, so I constantly felt a need to convey my gratitude. As time passed, I grew to feel that although I *was* technically in need, perhaps she liked that I was in *her* need. This made me feel like nothing comes for free.

I picked a table outside a café in central London and waited for Lucy. It was a lovely spring day and warm enough and dry enough for us to make the most of being outside (which is not very often the case in London). Lucy arrived and we hugged. We didn't

---

* Speak on behalf of the Asian experience.

acknowledge the time that had passed since we'd last met which I found strange. I had wanted to be her friend, it's how it felt at the start, but the relationship now was more a skills exchange. I was conscious that I stood out and did not resemble the people in her typical white, middle-class circle.

I was still trying to put the epic failure of my pilot behind me, so I didn't bring it up. Lucy had become famous* in the time we had spent apart, which made me even more self-conscious about wasting her time to help me with my material. Lucy didn't reference her fame, but there was always an unspoken understanding that she was better off than me on the circuit and beyond. I wish I'd known how to get it together myself and feel confident to launch my comedic voice without someone to bounce ideas off.

She smiled and we chatted a bit of small talk about her life and her friends and her week. The waitress came and took our order, I just asked for tap water. Lucy ordered a coffee *and* a diet Coke – I didn't pretend to understand, maybe it was indecisiveness! From our conversations, and my own experience at the Fringe, I'd gathered that comedy in the UK was about what was hidden away. I thought that maybe I needed to get more personal with my material. I was nervous about breaking my silence on what was in

---

* She'd had a 'good year' as it's known in the comedy world.

my closet (it was pretty full), but I'd been carrying it around for the longest time and wanted to broach the subject in my material, perhaps it was the key to unlocking the comedian in me, but first I needed to broach it at all.

Once the waitress was out of earshot, I confided in her my deepest darkest secret: 'My dad has two wives.' She was the first person I had uttered those words to and it took a lot for me to share that with her.

'Oh Sadia, your life's as good as a soap opera! It's just like *Eastenders* – you've got loads to talk about.' She was smiling and made big, dramatic hand gestures as she said this.

Now it could have been that she was trying to remain upbeat or make me feel better as I was in tears by this point, but it felt like totally the wrong reaction. I didn't know what I expected her, or anybody, to say, but that wasn't it. I was expecting an, 'Oh God, that's awful', or an, 'Are you OK?', at the very least.

I understand it was a catch-up to discuss comedy, but even so, it felt unusual to have my trauma trivialised in that way. Comedians are often jealous when someone else's trauma is better (or worse, depending on how you looked at it) than theirs. I understood that this was a world where sadness and pain were currency, but we were meant to be friends. We'd known each other coming up to five years. If my pain caused her this much pleasure, would my pleasure cause her pain?

I shuddered to think of what she thought of me – the way Lucy was so unsurprised by my secret appeared to validate both her perception of my culture and also seemed to validate how 'tolerant' and 'big a person' she was for helping me. Was that the way she saw me? Beneath her, flailing about in my victimhood? That was the final straw for me. I needed a more human or reasonable response to such an admission about something which was clearly so painful and personal to me. It gave me a new perspective. I questioned whether I was just a Brown person to her. Not me. Not Sadia.

Lucy seemed happiest when I gave her the opportunity to showcase how empathetic she was; when I laughed along to her jokes or agreed with her and played into her view of me as a pet project. But I wanted to be a comedian, not a charity case – though admittedly at my level there wasn't much difference.

Lucy was incredibly privileged and taught me to be just as entitled without appreciating that I wasn't like her and the same rules didn't apply to me as an Asian, a Muslim female without her connections. She convinced me for a while, that being 'BAME' would open all the doors for me. I foolishly believed her, even though I knew first-hand when I tried to find work this wasn't the case, no matter how popular the narrative had become. It is quite the opposite in comedy. I have to work twice as hard for everything I get, and even that is a humble amount, particularly at the beginning.

When we were by ourselves, Lucy would talk to me as an equal, but there were occasions in public she would approach me differently. Like when she introduced me to her other friends as if I was the friend in need who she really felt for. Often she would ask me to recount a story I'd confided in her about my experiences as an Asian woman purely, it seemed, for their entertainment. The crux of it was always about how she took it on, almost like it was *her* experience rather than mine. For instance, once we were at a party at the Fringe festival. Everyone was wasted but me and as we were leaving the balcony to go home at 4 a.m. a woman said to me, 'It's so cool you're Arab.' Lucy made a thing out of this, even when it didn't bother me, and the woman was clearly pissed as a fart. I hadn't expected a sober or insightful exchange with a complete stranger. I called it reverse code-switching* – although she appeared to mean well, I couldn't get a sense of her genuineness. It was like she enjoyed fighting this battle that wasn't even hers. It felt like I had gone from being her friend to a usable asset to her. I had to accept my place was beneath her rather than as her equal to maintain what we had. Life is full of hard knocks, with or without people like her. I was no longer the new kid on the block and even though I couldn't speak truth to her

---

* Where the speaker adjusts one's style of speech, behaviour and expression to optimise the comfort of others.

power, because I was made to feel like I was always wrong, I decided that I did not have to stand for this any more.

She did try and encourage me to look out for myself and not take on my mum's problems, but as being self-focused is so against my culture and upbringing, it made me defensive. After she'd dismissed my pain about my mother so blatantly, I didn't know how to feel. I discretely wiped the tears away and she changed the subject. I should have called her on it, but I know that she would have convinced herself she was right, so there was no point. She never spoke to me, but *at* me, like Ray J did. She was so steeped in my identity, she couldn't see anything else.

I realised that if I was willing to give up the parts of me Lucy didn't like or that didn't suit her perception of me, if I played into the 'oppressed' narrative so that she could help open doors for me, I would lose my own honest nature and sense of self. I hadn't got into comedy to earn favour or for people to feel sorry for me, I just wanted to be funny and make people laugh. I had so much more going for me than my 'struggle', even if no one else could see that. For all the money and exposure fraternising with Lucy could have afforded me, it didn't make me better, it left me operating within a narrower space creatively. I was already being stereotyped and contorted by so many things out of my control, like the media and my industry, that I didn't need that from my friendships too.

I walked away from that café knowing it would be the last time we would hang out, making the very difficult decision to disconnect. This wasn't easy as I felt incredibly grateful for all she had done for me at the start. I wouldn't have done my first show had it not been for her thoughtfulness and her help. Given the industry was about seizing any opportunity or platform possible, and who you knew rather than talent, it was as close to career suicide as I could have got.

That experience with Lucy confirmed what I had suspected all along – that it was rare to have friends in comedy. I wasn't special and eventually got replaced by the other BAME acts she assisted who were fast-tracked, going on to achieve big things.

I have my principles intact, and that counts for a lot – just sadly not to my industry.

19

A Few Good Men

After being in the comedy game for a while I needed to get an agent. I wouldn't be taken seriously without one and it wasn't possible for me to open the doors I wanted as an artist out on my own. Often television and network producers would expect communication via an agent and wouldn't deal with me directly.

What I lacked in confidence in the dating world, I made up for in comedy. I asked EVERYONE. I even approached agents that represented famous comedians; after all, I had nothing to lose. To my surprise, a few interacted with me for several months, that was until I pressed them for an answer, at which point the response was the same, they said no. A few others indulged me in small talk, to no avail. Most though were a big fat no upfront. No reason, just 'get out of my inbox'.

Although I was a pro at dealing with rejection it was such a battle. Each time I was filled up with the hope that my life might change, it would fall through and I'd be left questioning where I had fallen short. I was running out of options – the comedy industry in the UK was small and I was getting to the point where I'd pretty much tried everyone. I was determined though and kept googling. I came across GetComedy, an agency who looked after Jim Jefferies, an amazingly talented comedian who I rate a lot. I rang the number and got through to an agent called Chris. He listened to me, which was different, and agreed to consider me. We decided to meet at Grind, a place near his office.

Grind was an apt name because I was ready to grind. For a while I thought this was a bar or club where all the showbiz types danced the night away and he would initiate me into the dark world of comedy. When I came out of the tube station at Holborn and walked towards Grind, I realised, to my disappointment, that it wasn't a club but a coffee shop. Then it dawned on me, the only thing being grinded in there would be the coffee beans. I had put on my dancing shoes, these amazing multi-coloured River Island pumps, for nothing. But the work grind would go on. The café was full (I can't have been the only one trying to get my grind on),

Chris recognised me, and we squeezed on to a small table near the café entrance.

Chris is one of the most handsome men I have ever met in life, far too handsome for human beings, really. He was sporting a stylish quiff. He wasn't what I had expected at all. The thing that struck me was his work ethic. Comedy meant a lot to him. He was professional and supportive but said the usual stuff that I'd heard before, I had 'raw talent' (which I wasn't aware at the time is industry-speak for half-baked). He didn't sign me right then. He said he mostly represents live acts and that I was more of a writer. He left it open and said we would keep in touch. I felt a bit deflated which showed me it mattered. This wasn't a no, but it wasn't a yes.

A few weeks later, Chris came to see me perform live at a pub called Dirty Dicks in Liverpool Street. I worked nearby and after my nine-to-five, I waited around and prepared for the gig, which started at 8 p.m. I say 'prepared' – it was more of a pre-gig 'don't freak out' session. I was closing the first half and it was a mix of new and more established acts.

I met Chris by the bar and we sat at the back of the room. The show started on time so we didn't chat much beforehand. I went onstage around 9 p.m.; it was a large, well-lit room filled with about sixty people who were in great spirits. I felt positive and did my tried and tested material on Malala which they loved.

I got big laughs and I knew I had pretty much nailed the show. I came offstage exhilarated and eager to hear what Chris had thought of my act.

We went to Prêt afterwards and I had a hot chocolate. My adrenaline was so high, I spilled some on my hijab. I had never doubled up my hijab as a napkin before. Chris looked at his phone, he said he just needed to text his client Jamali* back. He told me about some of his other acts and the agency and we continued talking until the waitress told us they were closing. As we left Prêt, he turned to me with a smile. 'Sadia, I'd like to be your agent.'

I couldn't believe it! It was such a huge milestone for me in comedy. It felt like acceptance and belonging after so long being on the outskirts. Someone from the industry saw potential in me as a comedian! I finally felt validated, and it was worth the wait. I was ready for my cheque.

Although I didn't fully understand what having an agent meant in business terms, I felt relieved and hoped it would be the start of a new chapter for me. It was. Every comedian I've met since signing with Chris, has oozed with jealousy that he's my agent, so I'm exceptionally lucky. It may seem like nothing now, but back then in 2014, the industry was so behind in terms of being open to anything other than what was perceived

---

* The wonderful comedian Jamali Maddix.

as status quo, it felt exciting to be officially part of comedy. As an Asian comedian, it made Chris signing me, believing in me, mean so much more.

Chris had a smaller roster then and it felt like really being part of something at last. On any given day he was my Don King, my accountant, my life coach and my therapist. Chris came along to gigs now and again to support me and see how my act was progressing. I hated his support, or anyone's for that matter, as I had been on my own for so long I didn't want to grow dependent on it. The industry is so flimsy there is always the understanding that you could lose what you'd amassed and your relevance overnight. I may have hated it, but I was always thankful when he was in the crowd, he was always good vibes and being on the road and giving so much of myself could get quite lonely. I felt a lot of pressure performing when he would bring industry people along to see me, as I knew it had to go well and I didn't want to let him or, more importantly, myself down. I also hated having to impress strangers. I hadn't realised when I'd started that seeking to generate laughter was often interchangeable with gaining an audience's favour. I learnt that endearing myself to others actually went hand in hand with my job. Though eventually this made me grow as a person, I didn't love having to make a living off people's approval of me.

Chris came at a time when I truly needed it. I'd

never met anyone like him. A white guy who unapologetically tells it how it is. Chris was always vocal about
the things he liked about my material and projects as
well as the things he did not! Fundamentally Chris was
easy to like because he treated me as an individual first
and foremost.

I was lucky early on (four years in) and got spotted by
a producer who got me involved in a Ramadan short on
BBC iPlayer called *Things I'm Asked as a British Muslim*.
They were figuring out a lot on the day, so I didn't get
the script with my lines until the night before, and my
favourite scenes were cut. It was tough but the production company turned it out well. This BBC short was a
gift and a curse. A gift of an opportunity as it provided
exposure and served as a showreel. A curse because it
had turned up without much effort on my part, so led
to an expectation that everything else should also be
handed to me on a plate. That finally fame was calling.
I thought you just decide to be a comedian and then
do the shit comedians do.

As I still had a full-time job, I didn't put the hours in
at the beginning and then wondered why I didn't get
the call from *Live at the Apollo*. Before being signed by
Chris, I hustled quite a lot, thinking my ingenuity would
result in a breakthrough. I thought having a white agent
would finally take the pressure off as Chris would get
me there and my career would take off. What I wasn't

prepared for was the truth. Chris told me that I only had one shot at the industry and if I wasn't ready or good that it would set me back two to three years minimum. He gave me examples of other comedians this had happened to. They had gone for a big audition that hadn't gone well and then they were written off for a period of time – either until they had 'improved their act' or there were different producers looking at their material. It's such a small industry, news travels, there is no guarantee that a comedian will get a second chance.

I knew I had a good relationship with Chris because he was one of the few people from whom I graciously accepted bad news. I'd really only wanted to meet my favourite comics, but this was getting serious. I had to face the reality that I wasn't yet good enough to be put forward for screen tests, even after several years in the industry. The hard work was only just starting and I had to wolf down a lot of humble pie as I embraced what I knew all along: my so-called diversity or my hijab wasn't going to give me an upper hand. It was only work and perseverance that would see me through the finish line.

I was definitely not a perfect performer – I was slow at generating new material, and not as confident on stage as I needed to be. For now I needed to keep laying the foundations of my career, to keep building a future in entertainment, knowing full well it could amount to nothing.

Things I learnt from Chris:

- ♡ Don't reply to every email, certainly not on time.
- ♡ Some white people work really hard – I never knew this before working with Chris.
- ♡ Keep trying.
- ♡ I'm better than what people think I am.
- ♡ I'm not as good as I think I am.
- ♡ Don't try to impress people.
- ♡ Never give up.
- ♡ Keep the faith. Even when things don't pay off.
- ♡ Don't let anyone mess with my money.
- ♡ Believe in myself and have conviction. Look alive.
- ♡ Never wait longer than 20 minutes for someone to turn to a meeting. At 21 minutes you are entitled to never see return any of their messages.
- ♡ Grind.

20

He's Just Not That Into You

Things with Ray J remained stagnant. There weren't any signs that he would ever change. He was still reliably unreliable and, unsurprisingly, we drifted apart. I wish I could say this was because of a new-found resolve to love myself, but he'd simply stopped answering my calls or replying. I went to the gym to act like I was over him only to find out he no longer worked there, and no one could tell me anything else. He wasn't on any of the social media apps and so I had no way of reaching him. I wasn't surprised he'd decided to cut me off, yet I did think I deserved better from him. I had always been faithful to Ray J though we were never officially an item, but I knew now I had no choice but to move on from him. The only advice people had to get over someone was to get under someone else, which is easier said than done for me. I never really got over Ray J, partly because there was no one else to get under. This is, for the most part, down to me, I put everything into work and not a lot into relationships.

The industry is known to be the Wild Wild West. People are expected to be messy, flaky, high and the rest. If you aren't, you are the odd one out. The smiles are fake, the spirits are crushed and the morality is questionable. I consciously tried to distance myself from it socially which has been very isolating. It also meant that I wasn't involved in the dating sphere incorporated within it. I'd occasionally strike up conversations with comedians at gigs while waiting to perform. They described the comedy scene as 'incestuous'. It was like an orgy that I wasn't invited to. However the last thing I wanted was for people to think I've slept my way to the top. I wanted to earn my comedy stripes. But then, perhaps that is me self-sabotaging again; after all, where else did people meet partners than at work? Also, who is standing by waiting to typecast the hijabi as a slut?

Women on the circuit (who had slept around) would also warn me against seeing male comedians as they are almost always confirmed misogynists. Another unspoken rule I learnt early on was that I couldn't call comedians out on their shit because, more often than not, I would be labelled the troublemaker! I mean, who did I think I was? They were famous and trying to be funny, how could they possibly do or say anything bad? I had thought comedians were supposed to use our voices. Enforced silence is pervasive. Many of us know terrible industry secrets but there is no outlet. Without recourse to at least hold one another account- able, questionable behaviour is normalised.

I know from experience that some of the men on the circuit are misogynistic. They sometimes masquer- aded as if they weren't anything of the sort, but a lot of them hid in plain sight. In some ways being warned off them only made the prospect of seeing them seem more enticing. These women didn't go into much detail, which made things more curious: were they heartbroken or was it something more sinister?

I also didn't want to risk getting it wrong again as I grow attached so quickly. I found anyone vaguely inter- ested in me distasteful and unattractive. Men who don't like me, on the other hand – now *they* are my brand. I like having to work for it, knowing that I've had to earn a man's esteem. Though I do realise someone like that is probably trouble and no good for me, I have a way of pushing that concern right to the back of my mind. I like men a lot, and though I don't think I stand a real chance with a comedian, especially a non-Muslim, it is nice to dream.

In terms of my stand-up, I needed advice and guidance

with my new material so I asked a few comedians I respected for suggestions of people who had written good shows. One of the names that came up was someone that had worked on a show I really loved. His rate was affordable – about thirty quid an hour – so I contacted him. We agreed to have a few sessions and see how it went.

One of my meetings with Greg was at an American diner. It was retro, with a jukebox, exaggerated furniture and red booths. Greg was a skinny, edgy-looking white man, not somebody I would have ever spoken to had it not been for our comedy connection. I thought the meet-up would be more like work, and had come prepared with a notebook and ideas for the session. To my surprise it was more like a chat. We spoke about things beyond comedy and work, and he got personal about things that mattered to him. He declared, 'I think the way the country is run should be like jury duty. Every couple of weeks people from the general public should be selected to take charge so that we all have to play a part'.

I could tell from his conviction that this was from the heart and that made it so important, that it was his truth.

He was so gifted and he also didn't try and patronise me. He spoke to me like he needed no introduction, and just got me. It was almost as though he read my mind when he said, 'We want to use our powers for good'.

It felt like we were getting to know one another. I lamented, 'I'm never going to find someone, I'm going to be alone forever'. He called me out on this, 'Isn't that a self-fulfilling prophecy? You're never going to find someone *because* you're going to be alone forever?'

I couldn't deny that he had a point.

It almost felt like a date – for me, that is. Other than my one date at Yu Café with Ray J, I hadn't been out for dinner with a man. He was different to Ray J, he was the tortured-soul type and a musician in a past life. He had recovered from an illness recently, and his pain made him human and accessible to me in some way. I wasn't used to male company at all and it was such a treat talking about our shared interests. My fuchsia pink stilettos caught his eye, and he said, 'Wow they're something'.

The hijab didn't come up in conversation once which was a refreshing change for me, being myself. I would often squeeze in a meeting with him after work and gym where I'd been in trainers. Even though, I made a point of lugging around a pair of heels to change into for our session, I liked that he liked my shoes, and made sure I chose a different pair each time we met.

I didn't realise how good it could be, and suddenly I realised what I had been missing. As our meet concluded, he suggested that we should go to a zoo in one of our future sessions. I laughed out loud, this was the first time I found myself enjoying comedy rather than it feeling like hard labour.

I found myself thinking about Greg a lot after our sessions. He had already inspired me to embrace the lighter side of comedy more, by just messing around. I remembered his note, 'Go on stage and just dick around. Don't do material, just riff with the audience.' This was so daring and I felt energised. I'd clung on to the rulebook for so long, in all facets of my life, and this made me see things in a totally new way.

His humour was self-deprecating, and I admired his vulnerability. It was the strangest thing because I had always been into looks and interested in money. All he had was jokes, but amid the laughter nothing else mattered. I wasn't attracted to him, but he was really funny and when he made me laugh, I knew I had to have him. He had a reputation with women, which made me feel that if I was the chosen one, it would mean I was special. I know the saying goes that anything worth having isn't easy, but I'm not worth having and that's why I'm easy, and I wanted him.

I had never fancied a white man before. Growing up in East London around my community, it isn't seen as 'cool' to date outside of it. I had avoided white men given the differences in our values. They are full of talk, which is the opposite of Asian men, who have less chat but offer more commitment. I lamented that my options seemed to be fake love from white men or real hate from Asian men like Ray J. My culture makes the focus of partnerships on the more practical side of things, like running a household and family, and it felt like men with chat are too good to be true or that they are only after one thing.

Since guys never made a move on me, due to the well-known stereotype that as a hijabi I am supposedly sexually repressed, I felt it was my personal duty to flaunt my pussy to reclaim my sexuality and right this wrong. Greg seemed like he was always up for sex from the things he said. I even bumped into someone at a gig who said she was sleeping with a guy casually in an open-relationship-style affair. It wasn't until the end of the conversation that she mentioned it was him – small world. I didn't mention to her I liked him as it didn't make any sense to. I was against open relationships following my parents' ordeal. She said she was fine with it, but it felt like she was convincing herself more than anyone else. This felt like a loophole. Meeting him I could act out a date, under the guise of 'comedy', without any of the risks that came attached with actually being on a date.

Greg and I messaged each other informally and we'd moved on from working together to more casual meet-ups, where we discovered we really got on, so I thought the best way to let him know I liked him was to offer him sex. Which I did.

I texted him:

> I would love to have sex.

It was impulsive, which I wasn't very used to being with men. I also got bare excited when I liked a guy, as it was so rare that I found a connection. I know now that I got carried away. Maybe subconsciously I was trying to scare him away to solve the immediate problem he caused of giving me hope. He was taking up precious headspace so a reckless text meant I could go back to my comfort zone of rejection and continue my life alone. I didn't want to wait around and let things happen, after all I could be waiting forever. I felt like I had to seize the opportunity, in the absence of a moment to seize. I thought it was obvious when I liked a guy, which meant if I made a move, it shouldn't come as a surprise. If it wasn't obvious, it was even more important to make a move, I told myself. I didn't know what I was trying to say to him just that it was important to say it. It didn't make sense to be in such a rush given I did nothing else about finding a partner the rest of the time, but as these things don't come around often for me, I felt rushed to lay all my cards on the table.

Honestly, I didn't know what I would have done had he accepted my offer, I hadn't thought that far ahead. He replied immediately:

> You must stop this now.

I was stunned. I knew my text had been wild and uncalled for, but I had hoped he might have given me the benefit of the doubt, for being a comedian or being bad at this or something. I would never have done something like that, normally, which is why it meant so much. I felt ashamed, a feeling that I had promised myself I would never feel due to the damage it had done to my community. His rejection left me humiliated because I had never allowed myself to be so open as I was in that text to him. I even googled 'Can you die from embarrassment?' – the answer is yes, but it's rare.

A part of me knew my behaviour wasn't 'normal'. I went from zero to a hundred at record pace.* Guys are put off by my advances. They don't like me to chase as it gives the impression there is something wrong with me, but when I don't, they give it the, 'Women should make the first move as we live in equal times!' There is so much talk about how it is OK for women to make advances on men, but clearly not where I am concerned. The men I meet distinctly want to be the hunters, but it is like they've all gone on strike. My head gets so filled with conflicting expectations and advice – *what's a girl like you doing alone, you just need to put yourself*

---

* A couple of years after this, I left my Pilates trainer a Post-it note with my number on it. He moved to Australia shortly afterwards.

out there – that it wasn't surprising my own execution was so messy.

On top of that, I still hadn't mustered any self-worth. I wasn't taught how and had no belief in myself to cultivate this. Everyone had expectations of me and when I didn't fulfil them or broke out of the box messily, it ended in rejection, confusion and even aggression. I knew I made people uncomfortable, whatever I did, but I wasn't sure how else to be. I shouldn't have messaged Greg so outrightly, but I also wanted to see what might happen if I did. Perhaps it might be the moment a man would accept me for the full and complex woman I am or see me as a sexual being who fancied them and wanted to see if they felt the same? It might not have been the perfect way of doing it, but it was a shot in the dark I was willing to make for change. The rejection, though expected, furthered my feelings of self-doubt. I had hoped to move on from Ray J, but unbeknown to me, I had projected his entitled, clumsy approach on to the next guy. I'd made a mistake, but it was OK. I learnt from it that if I was going to throw myself at a guy in the future then I at least needed a plan and to know what I wanted out of it. I also couldn't expect every man to be pulled in simply by an offer of sex, even though none of my non-Muslim girlfriends had any difficulties in getting some when they did this. There was more to it that I was clearly missing. The less I felt I belonged on the dating scene, the more obsessed I became with the details.

How long after meeting someone could you shag them?

Why did relationships end?

How do you know when someone loves you?

What is the significance of the number of ex-partners you have had?

Why is there no sex in the champagne room?

Do you kiss with your eyes open or closed?*

Could I put a tracker on my man so I would know if he cheated?

How do you communicate you like someone without terrifying them?

I had a gig in Manchester that weekend. I put on a brave face and showed up all smiles. Being at gigs was another reminder of being alone. As a comedian, I travelled alone and then when I got to a venue either waited backstage or in reserved seating, alone. It was striking how inside I could be crumbling and yet it was my duty to raise the roof and make everyone else laugh. On the day Greg texted me back, those people would have seen me up on stage and never have realised I'd just experienced one of the most embarrassing exchanges of my life.

---

* Closed, of course, open would be crazy!

Voice note from Monty:

'Look, Sadia, when it comes to intercourse you know everyone has their own different ways to how they approach the topic, and if there needs to be more feeling when you choose to engage with someone that's perfectly all right. You will find the right man for you eventually who takes you for all that you are because that's what you deserve. Does it have to be a comedian? No, it doesn't. Does it specifically have to be someone in the creative industry? No, it doesn't. Because there are people who don't work in the creative industry that are creative in their own way. I think there just needs to be an attraction and a connection more than anything.

21

Supersize Me

I don't think you can be fat and be Muslim –
   that's from experience.
I *was* a fat Muslim.

When I was fat I didn't know if people ignored
   me because I was *fat* or because I was *Muslim*.
And actually what I found out is it was both.

But it turns out it was more because I was fat
   than because I was a Muslim.
I lost weight and some of the stuff I thought
   was basically islamophobia just dropped
   away.
People were less jumpy.

Maybe they don't hate the hijab-they hate cellulite.

I got into eating young. My father was a great cook. He would make huge pots of chicken biryani, potato lamb curry and tandoori chicken. My mum didn't enjoy cooking, which was strange to me because the stereotype in Asian households is for the mother to wait on the father. Both, however, would rejoice when I would show signs of hunger as though I had been nominated for an Oscar. They tended to use food as a way to show love, but also sometimes as a means of control. Later on, in my twenties, as I kept gaining weight I wondered if I could get a man to love me if I lost weight. I knew that the whole Muslim thing was a bit much for guys. I could feel how afraid both men and women were when I'd rock up. A mix of not wanting to say the wrong thing to offend me but also a pent-up fear that perhaps I might be eyeing them up as a snack. I was tired of being the person that everyone felt uncomfortable around.

I had been fat and Muslim for a long while, but when terrorism made me the triple threat, I had to regroup. Either I carried on living life as though I was a leper, or something had to give. The weight was the only option. One of my best mates, Davina, from the call centre, had joined Classpass. It is a subscription service to gyms rather than a membership to one, which suited me well given I wasn't good at commitment. Davina convinced me to join and though I found the prospect of exercise laughable I went because of her. Davina was really hot and had a hot partner too, so she was just doing it for health. As I never saw hot girls alone, I thought if I could get hotter, then I'd be undeniable. The magazines I'd see in the shops communicated this to me also. Cellulite? Disgusting. Fat rolls? Get rid of them! The fatphobia was everywhere I looked and the need to be skinny sank deep into my subconsciousness.

While I had initially hated the gym, I hated the office more, and when Davina left the call centre for pastures new, I continued training by myself. The gym served as a great escape from the monotony of the nine-to-five. Sometimes I went to the gym just to feel something, even if it was pain. I discovered a whole world where corporate workers would disappear to at lunchtime. Spin classes in nightclub-esque basements, and weight areas where men would yell like they'd just chopped down a tree. Strength training became my favourite as I found satisfaction from pushing metal, deadlifts to hamstring curls.

After I lost around two and a half stone, I did notice people were less stand-offish around me, which took a little pressure off. But lo and behold, guys never treated me any differently. They still didn't want to shag me. My little social health experiment proved it wasn't my weight after all, it was still the Muslim thing, or maybe just me. I had thought that being thin would make me happy. When I got thinner, I felt fatter in a way that I had never felt self-conscious of before even when I had been far bigger. I was happier when I was stuffing my face because I wasn't so hyper-focused on the alternative, and the things that did bother me just spurred on feeding. It was quite a U-turn, no longer having such an outlet.

Growing up all I had wanted was to be size 10. Now I had finally reached that arduous task, at the age of thirty, the goalposts had changed again. It was now the time of the curves, of the big bum and tiny waist. White popstars like Australian Iggy Azalea were appropriating the shape of ethnic women, and Asian women were not being represented in the body positivity movement at all. It was either be curvy or a size 8, or both. Either that or fake it with plastic surgery. Cosmetic surgery is forbidden in Islam, but I also feel strongly against it for other reasons. As a comedian I find strength in accepting who I am and resisting the opinions and expectations of others. In terms of my own appearance, I understood that it made no sense trying to please people as you couldn't please everyone. I also suspected cosmetic enhancements are prone to being addictive and it would be a slippery slope.

I now know it's not so much about what you look like on the outside, it's what you feel on the inside that really counts.

It sounds clichéd but I made the change to look like what I thought would make me happy, and still wasn't.

I'd made the change and still elements of my lifestyle were unhealthy.

I'd made the change and still men didn't suddenly drop to their knees for me.

You're better off embracing yourself for all that you are.

Having changed my shape, here is what I learnt:

- ♡ In some ways, I was happier when I was fat.
- ♡ When I was fat, people lied a lot to me that they didn't think I was fat.
- ♡ Body dysmorphia is real and often I think I'm bigger than I actually am.
- ♡ Guys tend to fancy girls no matter what size they are.
- ♡ How much you love yourself should not have any correlation to your weight.
- ♡ Intermittent fasting works, but some people need to eat small and frequent meals. It's different for everyone and you should find what works for you.
- ♡ Rest is important and will help get results.
- ♡ Burpees, like other bodyweight and compound exercises, are for the greater good.

22

It Happened One Night

You might think this isn't possible, but I was still trying to grasp what comedy is five years in. It was all rather mystifying. Chris, and other esteemed colleagues, would talk in grand sweeping statements and say they 'Saw glimpses of "it" in me when I was off-stage', that it was 'all in the eyes' or even (when they were a bit more honest) that I haven't quite got 'it'. Sometimes they'd say – in order to try and encourage me – 'it can be whatever you want' or 'maybe if you laughed more it would help' or 'perhaps try stand-up sitting down'. Ultimately it came back to 'You're finding your voice, feet, self, you need to focus'. They wouldn't usually say anything more concrete and so, to use a white people's expression, I was *flabbergasted*.

I didn't know what they meant by 'it' and I think the progression as a performer is basically figuring out what 'it' is. No one would tell me. I had to find out for myself, like the matrix.

I'd been with Chris a few years by this point and though he had started off getting me gigs, I learnt that this was actually my responsibility. He was an agent, not a diary manager. I started booking myself gigs through existing networks and using comedy groups online. Occasionally I got paid a free drink or next to nothing. I never felt like a loser because I had to be a loser to be in this world, for it was full of us. Dreamers and addicts, vulnerable and lonely people, and don't forget the predators and egomaniacs. We were all in an existential game of 'the biggest loser' and it was a test of resilience. I changed my approach and started doing the opposite of what I had done before. Instead of trying to get the best gigs and opportunities, I took anything I could find. I would email everyone I could about gigs and did lots of spots at a combination of new and less new material nights dotted around London pubs. There tended to be an audience of two or three 'real audience' members, i.e. non-comics, and then there were about eight comedians on top of that.

Comedians make for the worst audience as all we think about are our own jokes so we are too worked up to laugh. Either that or we've forgotten how. We are consumed by our thoughts on our own sets. The timing, pacing, delivery, punchlines, bits that work, bits that didn't work, new additions as well as the usual crap going on in anyone's head. We also don't want each other to do well because, of course, we want to be the ones to kill. Any comedian who says otherwise is a complete liar. There is usually one comedian in the audience who picks up the slack and offers a regular chuckle to support the act, who is getting nothing from the two or three audience members who looked stunned and are discreetly trying to locate the exit sign.

During this time, I started making jokes about my love life. Everyone loved them, so much so that the other material didn't even compare. My love fails led to comedy wins. I accepted how important authenticity was to me and my stage persona. I had to share more of who I was on stage to undo the narrative people expected of someone who looked like me. I wrote a set list about my love fails and the zero attention I got from guys. I went to a gig one winter's night in Brixton where I was closing the first half, which was like being the second headliner. The room was small but completely full, the audience about forty people. The lighting at gigs worked differently, sometimes they would spotlight me to the point where the whole room was blacked out and I'd be playing to an audience I could not see. Other times I could see the audience and had to compensate; this was one of those times. Although it may have been the two hundred-and-fiftieth time I'd performed my set, my job is to make it sound brand new and off the cuff.

I went on stage and started talking about how horny I was, as it had been forever since I'd got some dick. The audience warmed to my jokes and laughed along. I found my performance was divisive between the people who got it and laughed and the people who were self-conscious about whether they should be laughing at my material. I didn't really let that change the knowledge that finally I had turned a corner. I realised that audiences like it when I am myself and enjoying myself, rather than trying to perform for them. It was such a relief to find the voice I'd wanted to all along. I knew I had a long way to go in terms of being polished, but it was a huge first step for me to own my comedy and my talent. The more I practised and performed the material I wanted, the more confident I got.

It was a time of real development for me. I spoke with other more seasoned acts and realised how much work goes into comedy before, during and after gigs. I learnt way more from the gigs that didn't go so well than the ones that did. I learnt how important it was for me to enjoy the set as well as for audiences to. I didn't give myself too much credit for the good gigs because I felt I didn't have to work hard to bring them around, whereas the gigs where I could turn sheer indifference and apathy into roars of laughter and applause were euphoric. Depending on what was happening with life at the time, my performance would either come naturally or I would have to force it and it would be so off the mark. I wasn't always aware of what I was doing differently in the gigs that went better than the gigs that didn't. I didn't know how to operate the controls so that it always went the way I wanted it to.

On my own without anyone to bounce ideas off, I went through many periods of bombing. These weren't just at one or two gigs but could be for two to three months straight. I only realised six months later, when I did a gig that went well and the crowd had enjoyed it, that retrospectively I had been bombing that whole time.

There was one gig I performed in Greenwich where I was desperate for it to go well as I was trying out new material. The more I tried to make them like me, the more they pulled back. The crowd banded together and channelled their energy into willing me offstage. It then became a tug of war where either I won them back, which in a proper bomb meant just dying less painfully or getting destroyed. That night it felt like a draw as I'd managed to squeeze some laughs out of them towards the end of the set.

In the beginning, with the adrenaline and my nerves so high, it wasn't easy for me to detect a bomb, but as I got better at it and connected more with audiences, I could feel the energy and see it coming. As a comedian, I was operating on another frequency, I could tune into audiences in an intuitive, almost psychic way. I'd get so close to complete strangers, it was like we'd known each other our whole lives. Sometimes I thought I'd bombed but, in reality, had done all right. My natural instinct was to focus on what didn't go well as opposed to what did. A lot later, I realised that a sick part of me had enjoyed bombing. It was a form of self-sabotage and a way of maintaining control over the situation, a control I'd lacked in other areas of my life. If I didn't do well, that was to be expected, it was my fault. If you're on a high you can fall down from it, but if you're at a low, there's not much lower you can go, and that's safety in a way.

My first proper bomb had been when I had got a prospective agent to come and see me. It was a gig in Colchester and at the time I hadn't really gigged much outside of London other than at the Edinburgh Festival. The gig was at a nightclub, and I was the only one in a headscarf. Everyone was looking at me strangely, and as soon as I got on stage a lad yelled, 'Get your tits out!' I didn't think of a comeback fast enough, and as you can imagine, that was the end for me.

Doing my solo show in Edinburgh in 2014 to one solitary elderly gentleman at the back of a pub was another low, though it makes for a funny story. I had asked him if he could come back another day but he said this was the second time he had come back as the day before the venue had cancelled shows due to the rugby. I practically had to force him to make a donation afterwards and he reluctantly gave me a fiver.

I wanted audiences to like me so much and I even expected them to like me when I bombed – that they should like me simply for who I was. Eventually it dawned on me that I had to tell the jokes and not be the joke. As soon as I started treating comedy like a job, rather than a joke, I improved. What I learnt was that audiences didn't want nice. They wanted it as rough and in your face as possible. It wasn't about me being a Muslim or a hijabi, these things had no consequence, as long as I could sell the material and hold my own. When the comedy did come together, and I really connected with an audience, it was the best feeling in the world, even better than sex. But it would come at a price.

By the time I realised that it wasn't laughing and joking all the time, I'd already put so much into it. It was emailing promoters and introducing myself for the hundredth time, begging them for a five-minute spot at their remote, unpaid gig in six months' time. It was waiting in dingy attics/basements, that served as make-shift backstage areas and explaining how I pronounced my name to a compere. It was coming back to London from Scotland on the ten-hour overnight Megabus in the winter, trying to hold in going to the toilet so I wouldn't have to use the single, tiny cubicle they had that was always out of paper and handwash and had a suspect odour. It was during these moments I wished I had studied harder at maths. I was getting better and feeling better, but the majority of the time it felt like more trouble than it was worth.

Ultimately, I realised that this secret 'it' people would tell me about wasn't enough. There had to be hard work and trying, and if luck and privilege leaned in your favour, then you might be quids in. Chris would coach me, 'Nothing matters, it doesn't matter.' I had to learn how to stop caring so much, which was a completely unknown feeling to me. I was used to hard work, pressure and stress. I am the least reckless, irresponsible person I know. The shiny image of comedy was way past its sell-by date by this point. I knew I was in it for the long-run but the love–hate relationship was often more disappointing than Ray J had been. And that's saying a lot.

Comedians who changed comedy and changed my life:

- ♡ Patrice O'Neal
- ♡ Bill Hicks
- ♡ Chris Rock
- ♡ Sam Kinison
- ♡ James Acaster
- ♡ Katt Williams

It Happened One Night

♡ Norm MacDonald
♡ Dave Chappelle
♡ Richard Pryor
♡ Louis CK
♡ Bernie Mac
♡ Bill Burr

23

Nightcrawler

The day after the Westminster attacks in 2017, I got a message from Sky News.

> Sadia, we'd love to have you on to discuss your thoughts on the London attacks.

This was not the first of these requests I received. I was often asked to go on BBC Asian debate shows and news-based, non-comedy programmes to be a token representative. Chris was great. He never entertained them as he always affirmed that I was a comedian and not a token spokesperson. I was acutely aware that, being his only Muslim client, I was the only comedian who was asked for 'my thoughts' on these events. Maybe they should have thought about having someone like Harry Hill on to discuss terrorism, that might have been worth watching.

Sky News didn't want me. They didn't want a comedian. They wanted my scarf. My religion. My race. Someone to pluck from the ether to demonstrate how far-reaching their networks extended. The most audacious part of it is that they didn't want my thoughts at all. I had extensive thoughts on the subject. I was tired of the attacks and their consequences and the way they had impinged on our daily freedoms. I was exhausted by the Brown guilt of not being able to talk about it to white people. Of feeling like I should apologise for these acts that were in direct violation of rather than a proponent of my faith. But I could not apologise for I wasn't the person behind these acts of violence and, though I gravely denounced every single one, I was powerless to stop them.

I was saddened by the fear that became commonplace and the subsequent threats and the impacts these had on people trying to go about their lives. I felt for the people who had in one way or another had their lives or the lives of those close to them grossly interrupted. I was angry that it had cost me, and the Ummah*, our identity and I agonised at how the division this created played exactly into the perpetrators' hands. Threats

---

* Muslim community.

on our lives, both as British people and Muslims, had become a case of when rather than if and though no one said it, I knew that people felt aggrieved towards Muslims. Sky News wouldn't have wanted to hear any of this. They would have wanted a simple answer and solution, a reason and a cause.

Contrary to many white people's preconceptions, members of the Asian community in the UK are not wholly interconnected. It's comprised of diverse groups from different religions, castes, traditions and assimilations, there's very little informal community cohesion. I didn't feel I could be weak, even under these extreme circumstances. I couldn't lean on my community, as it was in bits itself, trying to hide its wounds and maintain a stiff upper lip. It was in a combination of shock, hurt and denial and couldn't afford to let its guard down for a second lest everything around it should crumble. I was paralysed by the loneliness this exacerbated between myself and the world that was already at odds with me.

I missed the small talk I used to share with white people that had previously made me gag – 'I love your scarf', 'When are you getting married?' or 'Do you have a recipe for chicken tikka?' I had always wanted to improve on the small talk, but I didn't realise at the time that that was as good as it would get as terrorism decimated these smallest of interactions. I would have done anything for someone to see me, to ask me even the most mundane of questions, like how I was feeling or what was my favourite TV show, anything! But with the rise of terrorism I was now invisible as people didn't know how to look at me any more, it was easier not to, and they certainly didn't want to compliment me or my culture.

So many groups couldn't see me.

Comedians didn't – I wasn't famous.

My family didn't – I wasn't married.

Asians didn't – I was open about sex.

White people didn't – they thought I was associated with terrorism.

Hot to average-looking guys didn't – I was a hijabi.

Feminists didn't – I wasn't a feminist.

My industry didn't – I was non-conformist.

My existence was such an inconvenience to so many. Everywhere I operated I was out of place. If I was on stage, I should have been at home in a kitchen. If I was in a kitchen, it was futile because I had no husband. If I was in the workplace, again it was jarring to those who didn't know how to interact with me. I went about my life as a robot on autopilot. I didn't stop to soak in anything, all I could do was keep going. I would work, gig, write, repeat. I didn't notice that through everyone not seeing me, I had stopped seeing myself. At some point I must have internalised the external hatred without realising.

These requests for comment compounded my sense of helplessness. I couldn't change people's views on the complex issues of race relations in the context of geopolitical ecoterrorism and evoke sympathy for Muslims, who were also hurting, in a two-minute segment before the sports and weather. I knew nothing I could say could offer any comfort and that anything I did say would hurt, divide or risk alienating someone. Though so much needed to be said, these people asking for comment weren't looking for a nuanced exchange.

And aside from all of this, I wasn't a political correspondent – my media training amounted to studying David Letterman's interviews on *The Late Show*. What did they want me to say? What would it change? No one wanted to voice their true feelings of anger and frustration about the climate of terrorism in front of Muslims and this made it harder. Nothing can be changed without listening. No one was doing any of that.

And so I continued on down that lonely street, and if anyone asked:

No comment.

24

No Country for Young Women

It was a Saturday afternoon and I checked into a hotel early. I was staying over in Scotland because I had a gig there that night. I received a call from Chris. He never usually called at the weekend*, so it caught my attention right away. He said he'd received a message from Elisha, a commissioning editor at BBC Sounds, enquiring about whether I had any pitches for a podcast. I said yes and he said he'd reply to Eli and let him know.

---

* White people are so chilled out on the weekends.

Chris Quaile
Sat 29/07/2017 15:36

To: Elisha
Cc: Sadia

Hi Elisha,

Thanks for the call earlier, I spoke to Sadia cc'd in and she would love to meet and discuss podcast ideas.

Would 2pm on Wednesday work for Sadia to come in and see you?

Cheers,

Chris

It was always a big deal to me to be considered for these things. I didn't want to get over-excited or be disappointed as, by then, there had been so many knockbacks – so many leads in comedy amounted to nothing. I had an idea that would explore what it was like being British when I didn't look British. It was like my voice didn't match my face and I found myself changing my attitude depending on who I was with. I would be quiet and well-behaved around family, fun and loud with friends and a pushover when it came to men.

I was asked to find a co-host for the producers to pitch the idea and it was obvious to me that it should be Monty. Not only did she have an interesting perspective, she has an amazing voice. A few weeks later, Monty and I got invited to BBC Portland Place, near Oxford Street, to discuss the podcast idea and to gauge our rapport as co-hosts. The production team, our first producer, Lachie, and his boss, Andy, in commissioning, developed the idea and it took their hard work and planning to get us to the stage where we could record a demo and then a pilot six months later. Recording the demo was one of the proudest moments of my career and to do that with my best mate was a dream come true. It went really well and it was the first time I'd ever been able to improvise and perform on a platform that was global! I couldn't believe it. It was so exciting.

Working for BBC Sounds as they were formed was fantastic. They were incredibly supportive and really wanted us to be ourselves and make it as authentic as possible. It was the first time I'd had such creative licence to do so since starting comedy. There were times before the launch and during the first few episodes where I really had to pinch myself to believe that it was really happening. I had been so used to being censored by television, due to my material being so near the knuckle, or being expected to present myself as a 'typical Muslim'. But this was beyond anything I could have wished for. Monty and I were given so much creative freedom and the network really cared about our voices and authenticity.

Eli had gone above his boss to pitch for us but he hadn't told me this at the time. It meant so much that they worked so hard to make the podcast happen. It felt like an incredible achievement for two ladies of colour to front an unapologetic, tell-it-how-it-is programme for the BBC. It was the best feeling being believed in and I learnt so much from Eli and the team of fantastic producers. Eli even said to me that I should write a book! Perhaps the most surprising thing I learnt was there are so many things I didn't know.

Being Asian, I had assumed I knew all there was to know about race. I was wrong. I remember us chatting with iconic British singer/songwriter Aluna over Skype while she was in LA. It was enlightening and revealing to hear her say she didn't feel she could tackle the subject of race in the UK, and she schooled us on the politics of the music industry. The podcast allowed me and Monty to meet so many guests from across the world and have really in-depth conversations that gave us insight into a world that I realised I hadn't even touched the surface of. There were so many stories and experiences, some of which I shared and others that fascinated me.

As the podcast developed it even had us on location. We took the Eurostar to Paris where we did a crossover episode with the French equivalent of our podcast, Kiffe Ta Race hosted by Rokhaya Diallo and Grace Ly. The French hosts explained to us how in 2018 the French

National Assembly voted to remove the word 'race' from their constitution, in the first founding article of the Fifth Republic. Parliamentary groups claim 'race' is ultimately an outdated term – which it is, but when racism still exists, race will. Diallo explained that this was done in the spirit of the French national motto, which is '*Liberté, égalité, fraternité*', which translates to 'Liberty, equality, fraternity'. This contradicted the astonishing accounts of discrimination we heard from French citizens who we spoke to on that trip. It even made me feel that the situation in the UK is better. But like Dave said, 'the least racist, is still racist'*, so don't get too pleased with yourself. However, the French wipe the floor with us when it comes to food! Bangers and mash wouldn't stand a chance.

One of my favourite episodes is when we spoke with Candice Carty-Williams about my favourite topic, love. She explained her reality of hustling, which of course I could strongly relate to. She was working a demanding day job at the same time she wrote her fantastic debut novel *Queenie*. We were also really humbled to be joined by the wonderful Jade Thirlwall from Little Mix. It was an amazing insight into her career journey and who she is as a person. She is such a strong woman and a huge inspiration.

We mixed humour with poignancy, and what was

---

* Lyrics from 'Black' by Dave, performed at The Brits 2020.

most striking was that many of our guests from the UK hadn't really had a chance to have these conversations around race, gender or class before. We were overjoyed that the podcast was recognised for Best New Podcast 2019 and nominated for Best Entertainment 2020 at the British Podcast Awards. It was hard at first because it wasn't stand-up and wasn't always about chasing the punchline, but I found my voice, and I developed a real passion for interviewing our guests. I found meeting others and hearing their stories and experiences fascinating, and it was nice not to have to always draw from my personal experience. Previously I had been so used to switching my demeanour around like I was on autopilot – here I learnt I wasn't the only one.

Career learnings:

- ♡ Practice makes perfect
- ♡ Be prepared, read notes/do your research
- ♡ Learn from your mistakes
- ♡ If at first you don't succeed, try and try again
- ♡ Listening to guests is your biggest gift, make notes if you have to, until it becomes a habit.
- ♡ Nepotism works. Use your contacts, and your contact's contacts!

25

Goodfellas

It was Friday night, and I was wrapping up work and getting ready to head to a gig. It was at a pizza restaurant in the heart of London called Café Mode. Its website boasts of prominent names – who all no longer perform there. Maybe it was a stepping stone to the big time! As I struggled getting on most bills in central London, it felt like a big deal landing the gig. I was booked for two shows, the 8 p.m. and the 9.15 p.m., and there was a break in between.

The room is a dark basement with low ceilings. It is quite small because of the tables and chairs, so the acts and I stood under the staircase outside the toilets, where a black curtain separated us from the audience. I didn't know any of the other acts on the bill that night. I think I let the gig get the better of me. With a few opening gags falling flat, I let the audience lead me, rather than leading them. I did averagely but they were a tough crowd. The other two acts didn't get much back from the crowd either. A new venue was always tough, but especially when you were competing with food.

One of the acts was a tall, medium-built fella named Hans, who wore glasses and was headlining the first show. I'd never seen him around before. We chatted in the break, and he mentioned he was trying to swerve a woman he had recently slept with who was really into him. 'Tall, albino and handsome. Gets 'em every time,' he boasted. He sounded like a dickhead; my interest was piqued. I immediately knew romantically he was the 'pretty boy or the brag artist' type. He went on last and did some material about the German army and riffed with the audience. He earned the respect of a medium-built, bald guy from Essex who had on sovereign jewellery and – as Hans established – was a 'hard geezer'. He did the least bad out of all of us which, in my eyes, made him a hero.

When he came back, I coyly told him, 'Well done.'

He chuckled and ran his hands through his hair. 'Thanks, it's one of those things, I guess!'

I nodded sombrely, thinking about how much I'd had to push for a small chuckle. 'They were hard.'

'You learn more from the gigs where you bomb,' he consoled in an air of overfamiliarity that I had grown to expect from comedians. The classic post-gig statement sounded fresh on him.

I was instantly attracted to him because he was tall. Something about tall men creates a powerful thirst in women that we cannot resist. It doesn't even particularly matter what they look like, because I'm not going to crick my neck to get a proper look at their face. I also liked that he was funny and took control of the situation. It was late after the second gig and we walked together along Covent Garden up towards Leicester Square. It was gone 11 p.m. and in the dark night the street lights and the odd star (with a hint of light pollution) were glowing. I wanted to know everything about him. I'd never spoken to anyone of his height before, he was at least 6 ft 2. There was something about having to tilt my head back that made me appreciate a man in almost an awe-inspiring way.

Hans told me he was German.

I said, 'What are you doing in London? Do they not have much comedy in Germany?'

Hans replied he was a man of the world. He liked to travel. He had just been gigging in Europe and was building an international following.

We exchanged notes about our favourite comedians and he raved about Norm MacDonald who he highly regarded. Typical white bloke, I thought to myself as

I'd never heard of him, but made a mental note to go home and watch all of his work.*

We walked past the shop Amorino. 'Let me get you some cake?' I offered Hans, ever the feeder.

He shook his head. 'No, it's late, but you can get me some next week?' He only had a week in London, but I was ready to buy him all the cakes in the shop.

Hans managed to get all the good gigs. He told me he was previewing his one-man show at Top Secret† on Saturday afternoon and then performing at the back-to-back late shows at Angel Comedy Saturday and Sunday nights. It was striking to bear witness to the fact that a foreigner was doing two/three gigs a night at spots that I wasn't even being considered for, not without at least being told there was a six- to nine-month wait, despite being a local act.

We agreed to catch up in the week. I was recording the podcast at Lantana Café in London Bridge the following Wednesday and we would meet after.

On Wednesday, I got ready. I wore a red PVC skirt, with a red top and my favourite false strip eyelashes. I took a selfie in a full-length mirror and sent it to him.

He messaged back:

---

* Norm is awesome; I highly recommend his set on alcoholism.
† A renowned comedy club in Holborn.

A thousand apologies, I got caught on a conference call, I can't meet you.

Who takes conference calls when they're on vacation?

I checked his website, he wasn't famous by any stretch of the imagination. I couldn't have been on his mind the way he had been on mine, which made this faux pas plausible. I accepted his apology and we agreed to reschedule to later in the evening at 6.30 p.m.

I waited for him by Embankment station. He turned up late at 7.15 p.m., which was frustrating because we both had separate gigs to be at for 8 p.m. He was doing one locally around Aldwych and I had to be back at Farringdon.

He kissed me on the cheek and suggested we took a quick stroll along Embankment pier. As we walked along, he looked me up and down. 'Your outfit looks hot,' he grinned.

I brushed over the compliment. I never quite knew how to accept one. 'I was recording my podcast today so wanted to make an effort. It was about polygamy.'

'Ah yes, you look so sweet, but your material is so filthy.' He recalled my set from the other night. 'You know Muslim men wouldn't appreciate a banging outfit like that.'

It was these types of observations put so coldly that were problematic. As a comedian I'd built a tougher skin and it wasn't a big deal as I'd almost gotten immune to them, and I knew there was an element of truth to what he was saying. While I didn't appreciate his lazy attempts at exemplifying insider knowledge of my culture, it wasn't easy to pick it up with him given I didn't know him. It showed he only saw me as a Muslim woman – first, before anything else. It made it difficult to determine whether that was a rational fixation or a curious preoccupation, something he wanted to conquer. I got the sense he liked the idea of banging me but with none of the hassle attached and what made it grubby was he sounded like it would be as a favour to me. Like he would be uplifting me from some profound, perceived oppressed state that he'd conjured up in his own mind. While I was desperately horny, a charity I was not.

He offered me a drink from Starbucks which I declined.* It was nice seeing him, but we'd barely had any time to talk before we went our separate ways. I had got him a selection of cakes from Selfridges as I'd promised and gave them to him before we said goodbye. Walking back into Embankment station, I felt both a little foolish and very disappointed. It was all too familiar. I'd really liked him but it didn't feel like that meant anything to him. He could have been Ray J, the similarity in entitlement and lack of substance was uncanny.

Even though I was sound of mind enough (just

---

* I was careful not to accept anything from men in case they expected sex in return. Which is strange given I liked stuff and I liked sex.

about) to understand that this probably wasn't going to go anywhere, the one per cent 'what if it did?' was enough to keep me interested. The idea of being happy, through the bliss of someone's acceptance of me and maybe even some affection, really put everything in perspective, and also made me lose all perspective. The sheer possibility of romance transformed me into another person. This made lust/love very deceptive as it was hard to discern whether it was the person I liked or the feelings that he invoked in me. At times it even felt like the attention alone was the drug because the little voice in my head insisted that I shouldn't be alone. I'm not a narcissist but it's a slippery slope.

I went on stage and performed decently which, in comedy, meant I was talking to the audience rather than presenting or delivering material. It's easier said than done. I didn't kill, but I didn't die. I could have tried harder, but my focus was elsewhere. It was a real problem that where guys were concerned, I was all in, so quickly, before there was anything to be attached to. It was something that I had got better at reining in, by blocking out hope and feelings, but I wasn't completely there yet.

Hans and I friended each other on Facebook. Later that evening, after I'd got off stage, I saw a message from him ping up on Facebook. It was a cute video of him taking a bite of the cake. I asked (practically begged) to see him after his gig but he said he was heading to watch one of his boys perform at a comedy show afterwards, which he didn't ask me to. I liked comedy too, but was he really choosing to watch comedy *over* sex? Maybe bromance is more powerful than romance. I didn't want to force it. It was 10 p.m. as I made my way home from Farringdon. I interchanged at Embankment to catch the District line and stared at my phone. By this point my excitement had long since fizzled out and I didn't feel attractive begging for his attention. That said, it had been a long time since I'd allowed myself to try. The last time was, thirteen months to the date, with my fateful message to Greg. I always seemed to reward myself for patience by overlooking the lessons I had learnt during that time and showing no regard for social conventions or myself.

To my surprise, as I was walking back to where I lived, he texted me asking to come back to mine. At that time, I was living in a horrific studio so I couldn't have him back. I lied and said my roommates would ask too many questions. I asked if he would meet me out and I was taken aback when he said we could meet on the London Eye where he could eat me out. I knew, from his lateness and general flakiness, all he wanted was pussy, but making out would have been enough and I didn't think I'd be up for getting my vagina out in the freezing cold. I had to stop and wonder if this was what I'd missed out on in my early twenties when

I was being hate-dated* by Ray J. Maybe I was glad I'd missed out if frozen labia was involved. I dutifully googled the opening hours as I was curious. I really craved male comfort, but alas it closed at 8 p.m. He kept stalling and I decided to continue home.

I texted him the next night – his last night in the UK.

He was very much of the opinion that if something was destined to happen it would. That was a very Islamic way of thinking† actually, but when it was 2 a.m., going on 3, it would have been nice to have some concrete plans instead of relying on destiny, an Uber to his‡ for example! The emotional toil of the anticipation and swift let-down had got to me. I was tired and called it a night once again.

That night I tossed and turned, contemplating how the men I liked couldn't even show me that they wanted me on a basic level, on a physical level. Whether this was out of their sensitivity towards me (or my hijab), it meant they left it to me to decide, and even then, sometimes they didn't reciprocate. It

---

* A relationship where to love someone you've got to hate yourself.

† Qadar (predestination) is one of the aspects of Muslim creed where we believe all that has happened and will happen has already been decreed.

‡ My girlfriends told me after that he didn't meet me earlier because he hadn't wanted to lead me on. They clarified that by trying to meet me at 2/3 a.m., it confirmed his intentions of it solely as a booty call and would have thus indemnified him from any blowback.

left me feeling kicked to the kerb because if they really liked a woman, they wouldn't let a good thing pass them by. I just didn't feel worth very much because guys never made any effort. Everyone is seeking human connection in some way, shape or form and, for me, I really needed to find it. I wanted someone to ask me about me. To be interested in who I am and my plans and dreams and desires. I had wanted more than just sex, and I hoped that Hans might be the opportunity for that kind of relationship, but he clearly didn't want that and so not meeting up with him again turned out for the best.

I woke up from a broken sleep at 5 a.m. and messaged Hans a good flight as he had an early check-in.

He replied:

> We had all the hours predawn. Next time it will be worth it.

I think by this stage (a girl who he had only briefly exchanged passing conversation with twice), he probably had me down as a nut job.

I had to consider that maybe he was right. I was displaying qualities and taking actions which showed that my mental well-being wasn't the strongest. A little while after, once my bruised ego recovered, I realised that, like comedy, love is as much about the things I didn't do as the things I did. Sometimes onstage, it was the things that were left unsaid that lingered. Even the times I didn't always believe in myself, I didn't jump on to a stage begging and demanding audiences to love me, and I absolutely never would, *imagine!* Instead I had come to a point where I was contained in my performances and self-confident. The times I tried too hard to impress audiences it never worked because the power this gave audiences corrupted them. There were shows where I had given it my *all* and they didn't strike a chord for whatever reason. But I didn't mind the shows that didn't go well when I had done my best. You can't win them all. Perhaps I wouldn't have so many regrets when it came to men if I accepted that my best was enough.

It was my desire, to love and be loved, that I had to contain offstage. To be myself around a guy I liked, minus the desperation. If we hit it off, great, but it wasn't about making a show or a fool of myself. This took worth from me, for nothing. I didn't have to give it all up before we'd even been on a first date. Giving my all would mean nothing to the wrong person. When it's the right man for me, I won't have to try so hard, because he will just know.

Voice note from Monty:

'Sadia, why does it have to be a comedian you specifically have to be with, surely it's whoever tickles your favour or who treats you right? And as for that guy, you know what I'm going to say about that, what is the point of trying with guys like that? What is the point? You need to elevate higher. If this dude was interested in you he wouldn't have been so dismissive of you.

'Like you're not a plaything, not unless you choose to be. Sometimes I choose to be a plaything and I enjoy it but you're not a plaything. Allow that guy. I don't rate the people that you fancy, I really don't. Because they're not nice to you and I personally don't think those are how romantic connections should be.

'For example, you know, I was on Hinge recently and my ex messaged me. Now, this is the dude who had different girlfriends on different continents, London but Cape Town too. Can you imagine having different girlfriends on different continents . . . he really thought he was doing me a favour. He wasn't, which is why we weren't together for very long.

'He texted, "Why don't you come and see me?" And I said, "No, thanks." He replied, "Oh yeah? But you used to come down and drive down and see me all the time." I said, "That was a long time ago."

'Just because he showed me a bit of attention, I don't have to go running, I should jump from here to south-east London . . . he is very mad and so are the people in his village. So you shouldn't have to go running for just anybody who hasn't earnt it.'

Goodfellas

I recently discovered I'm into foreign men!

That's white guys innit.

I actually fuck with white people.

My agent's white, my director's white, you're probably white.

But white guys see dating me as a challenge.

As if by fucking me they're fucking the whole community.

Like they're invading Iraq (gestures to vagina) again.

And people judge you when you date outside your race.

They would think I was with a white guy for his money.

And that's true.

That goes for any man I'm dating.

What I'm saying is I eat ass, and that's got to be worth a pair of shoes or a bracelet at the very least.

I do it sober, so it really counts.

26

White Mischief

I was asked to perform at the first ever Asian Women's festival in Birmingham. It was an all-day event and I got to meet the crowd throughout the day either informally or during some of the seminars. The attendees were mostly of Asian British heritage and spoke of the same themes I had been discussing on the podcast since its inception. It was one of the few instances I didn't feel so alone in my experiences, surrounded by incredible Asian women from all faiths, backgrounds and walks of life. It consoled me that we had come a long way and things were changing for the better. Having learnt about how bad it is to be judged before anyone knew me, I thought it only right to give every audience a chance in return. I didn't think about the many failed performances in front of exclusively Asian audiences in the past. I hoped to have learnt from them and win over the people who were there to have a laugh. That day I did my set in front of six hundred Asian women and they loved it! They laughed, gasped and cheered. It filled me up till I could burst. I felt so connected to the Asian women in the room.

As well as performing, I spoke on a panel about broadcasting. I explained what it was like getting my big break with the podcast and working on being authentic even though that may not always be what was expected or wanted. It went well and it was exciting to see so many Asian women looking to embark on a similar career path, which wasn't something many Asian women like me growing up would have even considered. Then it came to the Q&A and a beautiful twenty-two-year-old Asian woman stood up shyly and asked me, 'Is it all right for me to date a white man?'

I understood the question perfectly. She had been seeing a white man and things were beginning to get serious, hence the question. She didn't know what she could or couldn't do with her sexuality/life and she said she could not discuss it with her family. This was very familiar to me. I could understand her hesitations towards veering against convention, it was never an easy thing to do. The desire to date within our culture and ethnicity is not a catch-all for the Asian experience though, and I had a few Asian female friends that were divorcees who, in the interest of not being banished from society, told me they were encouraged by their families to even consider white guys. Notably remarriage was not for their happiness but rather as a step towards societal redemption. White guys were seen as easy, safe, dependable, or in other words vanilla. The perfect safe bet especially for someone that had been bitten before. There is also a lot to be unpacked about the support of moving into dating people of a lighter skin colour, rather than darker.

One thing Asian women have to factor in is that there are a lot less Asian men proportionately to Asian women. The mortality among Asian men (notwithstanding the jihadi body count) is not great. Therefore, if marriage is a priority then dating outside of the race may have to be a real consideration so they can stand a chance at all. I often found white men understated and emotionally inhibited. How much of me would be about my culture to them? Would they think everything I did was 'playing the race card' or could they separate me from my race?

My response was, 'Go on and get that white dick!'

The audience let out a roar of laughter though I was deadly serious.

I went on to say, 'If it's what makes you happy and what you want, it's what you should do. You can't spend your life trying to people-please your family, community or friends.' She sat back down. Young girls like us are so used to being told no,* and though I had absolutely no authority, I hoped what I said provided her some comfort in feeling understood without being judged. It felt as though she had already made the tough decisions alone anyhow.

I didn't see it as 'lesser than' to date outside my race, I was in the right country for them after all. But what did I even know about white guys? There are no stereotypes. Did they have big dicks, small dicks? Did they snore a lot? Was their favourite food coleslaw or mayonnaise? What was their obsession with *Star Wars*, *Doctor Who* and sci-fi about? We know that Asian men suffer from a high risk of heart disease and fundamentalism, but what are the risks with dating a white guy? Also, what is it about me that they found attractive? Were they longing for a submissive homemaker? Did they have an Asian bride fetish? Was it the lure of the unknown? Or now that diversity seemed to be more of a trend, was it because I passed for cool? Asian men who I'd come across at work would say, 'Conquering is in white people's blood', which suggested I couldn't amount to anything more than a conquest.

In a world where Asian women are amassing success

---

* For those who had started relationships and want to get their parents' acceptance retrospectively. I think the remedy for these situations, where gaining parental approval mattered, is to try and have more conversations with the family touching on this.

and defying stereotypes it feels like a foolhardy, self-imposed limit to stubbornly decide not to date outside my race. If I found myself in circles where the opportunity presents itself, why not? I would just be sure to consider what I would and wouldn't compromise on before it got too serious. I've had both Asian and non-Asian men tell me they're into 'Indian girls'. If this is the first thing they had to say, it is cringy and also mystifying. What do they mean by this? Is it our skin tone, demureness, tight vagina or subservience? Without 'Indian girl' being clearly defined it's hard to discern – and as someone looking for dick it's important to know – to help consider what to amplify and downplay. I ultimately feel if someone says they are into [*insert whole ethnicity of people different from their race*] then they are likely to have some deep-rooted issues and fetishising tendencies. That being said, if an Asian woman chooses to use it to her advantage, I can't judge or say I wouldn't do the same. Ultimately, dating shouldn't be political even though so many make it out that it is. It's important to clarify, that's not to say your politics shouldn't be aligned with your partner's, but it's more about following your heart and finding someone who you connect with.

I know Asian guys, regardless of whether they wanted to sleep with me or not, didn't want to be seen with me. It is the opposite problem white women have of not wanting to be trophy wives. These fellas are reluctant and at times ashamed to put it out there. I was willing to accept being a 'secret' with them where I would not allow that to happen with a white man. Asian women typically hold on to tradition and cite this as a reason for gravitating towards partners of the same race. It certainly isn't religious tradition as Islam does not differentiate or show preference towards one race over another. They may have meant that the same race is their type and, if so, I understood that. As for the idea of dating within my own race being 'tradition', the point is that as a collective, we have been taking baby steps away from tradition for decades now, we just haven't owned up to it because it's not palatable to us, ironically, due to tradition!

Asian women are working, Asians are having long-distance marriages (husbands working abroad usually) and we are anything but traditional in many senses. Yet still we long to be revered as operating within the boundaries of tradition. Why? So much of tradition and culture is transient. What is it we are afraid of that committed us to behaving a certain way and repeating what is, at times, misguided patterns of behaviour? Couldn't we move forward embracing what serves us, and rejecting what doesn't?

So much of tradition makes very little sense, particularly in the present day, and there is little by way of explanation for the reasons behind it – so much of what we do is to keep the parents happy, to keep kinship happy. I wonder if this is why so many Asian mother-in-laws are such bitches.* Because they were never entitled to their own happiness, so the only thing left is for them to snatch at others. I'd never seen a happy mother-in-law. Not once. I've never seen a secure and content mother-in-law that made me think to myself, 'I want to be just like her'. I probably never will. Every mother-in-law I've seen epitomises the opposite of what I want to become. I don't want to be bitter and lonely and only find purpose from the act of keeping other people's heads down.

I always wanted a serious relationship over a fling and my fear of dating outside my race is that it would only be something casual. In my culture, we're told that 'you leave a bit of your soul' with whomever you fuck. It left me contemplating whether I would be trading some of my Asian for his white? As a child of an immigrant, hadn't I already made that trade? White guys struck me as emasculated. They had power but they were also riddled with guilt and indecision. Being a red-blooded woman, I want a leading man, not a supporting actor. When I was younger, I watched a porn film of a white guy fucking an East Asian woman, he

---

* You would hear the most brutal stories about mother-in-laws. I remember one someone told me that the mother-in-law didn't like her daughter-in-law and put cyanide in her shoes which burnt the soles of her feet.

cried right before he came. To say this put me off is an understatement. It made me think that, sexually, white men hold lower status than ethnic women, so while socio-economically seeing a white guy might be dating up, it would definitely be fucking down. If my interactions with people who are unfamiliar with Islam and the hijab were anything to go by, I could see dating outside my race/religion being cumbersome. Given I long for a partner who is psychic I wouldn't be thrilled about being somebody's personal tour guide into Islam/Asian culture.

As a child, I would hear men of all races sniggering about the infamous *Asian Babes* magazine. There are some English men with a penchant for Asian women mainly because they're more traditional than white women. Whether they are introduced to them through assisted or arranged marriage services, or find her themselves on a trip to Thailand, the idea of having to live up to pre-dated stereotypes turned my stomach. I didn't want my skin tone to be an indicator of my sexiness, but then it was the same with trying to dispel the fact that I wasn't unsexy due to my faith. I want to be seen as sexy for me, because I am Sadia Azmat with a hot bod and great personality, not for any other reason. On one level dating someone of the same race is as close to 'equal' in a relationship as I can hope for. I don't ascribe to the caste system, I don't even know my caste, so I wouldn't be involved in the one-upmanship that can creep in with other relationships. While there may be class differences, if there was any self-hatred, it would be balanced out because we would essentially be equivalents of one another. Of course, dating anyone, regardless of what we have in common, isn't without it's compromises and follies.

On a primal level Asians understand each other. That's good and bad. Innately Asian women didn't know how to feel good about ourselves. It's a recent thing we have begun to explore and indulge in, but to date, we've mainly found happiness in facilitating joy and contentment for others, to our own detriment, with an afterthought of being recompensed in the hereafter. The queens of not creating a fuss, not knowing how to be loved, when love is all about fuss. It is easier dating within the same race because of the 'known variables'. I know I am getting a circumcised penis. I know that he would rather lie to his mates about being single than introduce me to them. I know he probably wouldn't introduce me to his parents, but that was OK; after all, unless we are talking nuptials, Asian parents don't really want to know. Frustratingly this makes it easy for some Asian men, to whom not giving me joy was both familiar and convenient, to take advantage of my 'low maintenance'.

In 2017, during the time I was recording the 'No

Country for Young Women' podcast, I was often a guest on my good friend Mobeen Azhar's show on the BBC Asian Network. One episode the topic of discussion was attitudes towards interracial dating. Most of the (Asian) callers who rung up in that episode confessed their parents would have an issue if they dated outside their race. The only exception to this was marrying into wealth. I'd had many conversations with Asian men who had said they would view me as 'soft' for going with a white man and loose for dating a Black man. It is perceived as a shortcoming as it implies that I couldn't 'handle' an Asian man. Men would regard it as treacherous, to the point where it would almost forfeit me my race! I'd be held in contempt, for breaking some farcical convention. Likewise, certain women would view me with contempt, seeing this as a move against my culture entirely. The notion of love is regarded as foolish and doesn't move a lot of Asians, who are steeped in antiquated and historic legacies.

Being a sex-positive and unapologetically loud Asian female stand-up comic, I don't care what people think about me dating someone from outside my race, that is the least of my concerns. It's my life and I am the one who has to deal with the consequences of my decisions, no one else. If I happen to be a different colour to my partner, I could make it work. It is about how we could come together as one. I would never rule it out as love is anything but straightforward, but I know that this person would have to be pretty special and sometimes I question whether that even exists. It isn't out of some misguided sense of loyalty to my community. The skin colour of my partner is minuscule in the grand scheme of things. It is more about whether they can see me for who I am as a whole.

I worry, in the same way the girl who stood up and asked me if it was all right dating a white man at the event probably felt. I know that I would be a different version of myself if I dated a white man. I can't say who that would be, and that it wouldn't lead to growth and betterment, but I would check myself on topics where there isn't shared understanding. Maybe this would be to avoid the fights or out of fear that he wouldn't accept all of me. In Islam it is permissible for men to date non-Muslims, however Muslim women are not able to do the same as the kids needed to be raised Muslim and therefore it is a requirement for the male role model in the family to be Muslim. Women are encouraged to marry someone for their faith. This is the main obstacle for me considering a non-Muslim for a partner. Although in recent times, Islam has had the highest rates of reverts seen in Europe, it's asking someone to make quite a personal commitment. Ultimately, I'm asking them to trade their soul for my pussy – which I think is a worthy trade – but a combination of pride and low self-esteem prevents me from asking this much of someone.

I wonder still if that young Asian woman is happy. I hope so. As long as both people in a relationship are fulfilled, no matter what their race, that's what is important. Life's too short and there were too many bad options to let the potentials slip away just because they don't season their meat.

27

I Know What You Did Last Summer/
There Will Be Blood

I was bored and frustrated one night and googled Ray
J. His mobile number popped up. I hadn't transferred
my old contacts when I got a new phone and so I didn't
have it. It was like candy to a baby; I couldn't believe
it. I stared at those eleven digits, wondering whether
this was fate or if I should leave it. I could hear Monty's
voice in my head cussing me out for even considering
messaging Ray 'The Punisher' J. But I could also feel
my heart pick up speed and I felt more alive than I
had all week in a hot and dry London.

And so, I sent him a text, against all better judgement, and with big 'Hey, stranger' energy.

> I'm thinking of you.

> Who this?

So he'd deleted my number . . .

> Sadia.

I was living in one of the smallest studios imaginable at the time. It was a self-contained box, thirty square metres on the eighth floor of a converted commercial block in Newham, East London. It was cheap but the size of it barely held my belongings and I felt suffocated most days. In such a confined space everything felt so much more magnified – my thoughts, worries and problems. I needed escapism and comfort and after a few sexts, Ray J came around.

Sex with your ex is good but I don't recommend it. It's good because it's new and yet familiar. I don't recommend it because it never comes without hassle and it's inevitable that you'll realise you're both in different places. It kind of knocks the shine off the memories you had (not that my ones with Ray J had any). The boundaries are also undefined and clouded due to years of history. Should you pick up from where you left off or should you be slow like new lovers? The sex was enjoyable, I was present. I didn't think much more about it afterwards. I didn't delude myself that it meant anything else to him, or that it could lead to anything. He was who he was, and he wouldn't change or become a better person because we had sex again.

But a couple weeks later I noticed my period was late. It was always on time every cycle, somewhere between twenty-five to twenty-nine days, it would be thirty-one days at the most. It had been thirty-four. I thought it might be normal and busied myself with going to the gym, thinking that might spur it on. But no, nothing. I was uncharacteristically chirpier for the time of the month too but I put it down to the acupuncture treatment I had received that had been effective at easing my symptoms of PMS.

After a few days of putting off thinking about it, I suddenly remembered what Ray J had whispered post-coitus. 'I've cum inside you,' he'd said. Still, I mentioned it to him, and he said I should take a test. I genuinely thought he was being silly; my period wasn't that late. But I went down to Superdrug and got a Clearblue pregnancy test. The instructions said it was best to take it in the morning. I was 90 per cent sure it was a waste of time. But the next morning I woke up, peed in a plastic container and dipped the test in it.

After a couple of minutes, it told me I was pregnant. Three weeks pregnant.

Shit. This was one test I wish I had failed.

My breathing started to get unsteady and my skin prickled with sweat. What was I going to do? One lapse of judgement getting Ray J round. Pregnant. The consequences of my own actions were a hard pill to swallow.

I texted Ray J a screenshot of the test. His response:

> Book an appointment to see your GP.

That was all. It was obvious what *he* wanted and he clearly wanted me to sort this quickly. I was shaken up and I checked with him a few times to see if he was sure that's what he wanted. Ray J replied he already had his own amazing kids and was sure. I hadn't wanted kids. But I had never thought I would be in this position, doing away with one – my kid. I had never had the longing to have babies that other women spoke about. I was a stand-up comedian – my life was a sequence of masturbating, writing on the back of my hand and travelling long distances to gigs. From what I knew of parenting, it was a lifelong commitment. I couldn't see through an entire boxset, I didn't do commitment.

Ray J's coldness was the final nail in the coffin.

I went to see my GP. I wish I hadn't needed to, all she did was give me two phone numbers for different abortion centres and marked it on my file that I wasn't having a baby. She wasn't mean about it or anything, but it made it real, telling her. It made me feel guilty for not keeping it. I couldn't believe I had got myself into this and it felt like a huge blow. I really wish it hadn't happened. I'd never conceived before, and suddenly I felt differently. I can't explain it. I didn't know what it was – whether it was the chemical changes or the baby's way of trying to make it – but a part of me wanted the baby. It would have changed my whole life. I'd be a single parent, yes, but I'd have something to love. All these romanticised thoughts didn't take into account the reality though. I didn't want to do the grind. I was already thinking about babysitters and ways to get away from the unborn child if I needed space or to focus on my work. Ray J's words echoed in my head, 'If you have a baby, you raise it yourself, you don't enlist babysitters, that's not what real mums do.'

It wasn't that the time wasn't right, I won't fool myself. It was that I wasn't right. I would sometimes wish I hadn't been born and what if I passed that on in the genes to my child? Or maybe that was just my way of excusing the fact that I was about to do something awful. Something un-Islamic.* Something I didn't blame others for doing but wouldn't be seen dead doing myself. Having an abortion. I had to believe my child would be messed up in order to push myself to go through with the act.

I rang up the first abortion helpline hoping there

_____

* In Islam, where an abortion is required, it should be as close to conception and not any later than the end of the fourth month. This is because it is stated that the soul enters the body at the end of the fourth month. If within these timings, certain opinions rule the procedure makruh (disliked) rather than haram (unlawful) (Dr Bilal Philips).

might be a same-day appointment. The sooner the better. But that's not how it worked. I got through to the call centre officer and thought immediately how that must have been a horrible job. Imagine trying not to say the wrong thing all day and speaking to incredibly vulnerable women day in day out. Trying to be clinical and not involved with the feelings that were basically pouring through the phone. Not being able to laugh or show any emotions and just being as invisible as possible, a quiet facilitator to the process. I stumbled yet maintained the urgency, 'Er, I need to book a termination.'

'We'll need to get you to speak with the nurse first,' the man at the end of the phone said indifferently. I recognised the ambivalence as I would often dish out these passive, scripted, robotic phrases at the call centre, I was well-versed in them.

I felt stressed. 'What do I need to speak to them for?'

'It's part of the process, I can book it now, but you would need to speak with them before your appointment.'

I didn't like the elongation of such a painful process but I knew it wasn't worth arguing. 'OK, that's fine.'

'I'm just going to take some details, what's your favourite colour?'

I couldn't believe what I'd just heard and choked. 'Um, sorry, did you say favourite colour?'

'Ah yes,' he replied a bit sheepishly, trying to maintain the solemnity with which the question had been asked. 'We need to know to set up your ID in case you call back.'

I couldn't think and blurted out, 'Purple.' It wasn't my favourite colour. I wondered who was having abortions by impersonating someone else.

He gave me my security code for future reference and confirmed that he had booked my appointment for three weeks' time. I couldn't believe it. Three weeks? What was I going to do in the meantime, bond with the baby? Change my mind? I called the second abortion number and booked a second abortion, just in case there were any issues with the first one. As a backup. They didn't bother asking me for my favourite colour. And that was it. That is what I would have to do.

The same day Monty and I were recording the finale of the first series of 'No Country for Young Women'. I didn't tell her, I didn't want to tell anyone. My agent, Chris, rang me coincidentally as I walked out of Lantana Café, where we had just finished, and I was making my way to the station, brain frantic, but trying not to show the world I was falling apart.

Chris sounded perky, 'Hey, Sadia.'

I tried to reflect his voice and tone to disguise my real feeling. 'Hi, Chris.'

'How are you?'

'I'm fine.' I was always fine. I couldn't be anything but fine because I just had to be. I've always wondered what people would do if you responded to their 'how are you?' with the honest truth. It was like an unspoken rule where you can't reply with your true feeling.

'Well done on the second series, that's amazing. Maybe we could celebrate if you're around tomorrow?' Chris was always so thoughtful, and while I appreciated it so much, I couldn't face it.

'No, I'm not. I've got a gig tomorrow,' I shot back, clipped and blunt.

I could tell he was worried about me but didn't want to pry. 'Are you sure you're all right?'

It was in that moment that it all came flooding out of me, the emotions, the fear, the uncertainty, the guilt, poured through the phone. 'No, I'm not. Chris, I just found out I'm pregnant. I took a test this morning.' I told him everything I was feeling, I was disoriented. I hadn't planned on telling anyone, but it was more because I had no one to tell.

Chris started responding but there was so much traffic I couldn't hear him. He sounded shocked. When I finally could hear him, he said, 'You've got yourself into a spot of bother, haven't you?' – which might be the most British response to anything ever.

All I said was yeah. I was at an all-time low. It always felt like when something would go well, something even worse would happen, almost as a punishment. There was always a price to pay if I had good fortune. I wondered why I couldn't have peace for all of five minutes.

Chris spoke again, 'Sadia, why don't you come and meet me for a coffee tomorrow and we can chat.'

I huffed, frustrated. 'I don't really want to, I have a gig tomorrow.'

I could sense his surprise about how I wouldn't shift plans even when something like this had come up. This was my coping mechanism always, I had to keep going. It was all I knew and it saved me from having to face up to what was going on. I needed my brain and body active and busy.

Chris insisted, 'It's fine, you can meet me before your gig. We can just chat. You don't have to talk about it if you don't want.'

This wasn't comedy, Chris couldn't make this 'go away' the way he could handle other problems that came up. He was always strong for me. Telling me not to worry about the gigs that didn't go so well and re-assuring me when things got tough, but in this situation, I felt completely out on my own. Despite this, I reluctantly agreed to meet him the next day. Sometimes I thought Chris was too good to me. I mean, I didn't really see what was in it for him. Based on the work I amassed he hardly made a dime of commission from me and so I never really wanted to put him out. But he was better than an agent, he didn't just see his acts as products or comedians, but people. He was so good at seeing things I couldn't.

The next morning at the flat, I got a call from a nurse.

After she took some details to confirm it was me, she tried to ascertain why I was having the procedure.

'We need to understand if it's financial reasons, psychological reasons or something else.'

It felt like I was on a strange episode of *Who Wants To Be A Millionaire* without any of the lifelines. I didn't know what to say. I was wary of saying psychological as I have a family history of mental illness and there is always a stigma with mental health in my community. It wasn't financial either, but in the absence of other options I just said, 'I'm not ready to have a baby. I wouldn't know how to look after one. I don't have any family to support me.' She seemed to accept that.

I met Chris at Soho House in Dean Street that evening. I always felt self-conscious going to members' clubs, which is where I would often meet people from my industry, be it producers or directors. They are aspirational venues and what the 'members only' always symbolised to me was that it was a place where my sort were not invited or welcome. It was an exclusive place because it kept the so-called riff-raff out. I never felt right whenever I would go to these places. Even though my name was always on the guest list, I still needed a white person to vouch for me.

I met Chris on the first floor, he was in a corner, and we hugged. We talked about the new series of the podcast and other bits and pieces before I had to go to the gig. I could tell Chris was trying to cheer me up.

He wished me luck and I went on my way. We didn't speak about the pregnancy or what I would do, but I appreciated him trying to distract me.

I didn't really take good care of myself, being a jobbing comic, and so my brief stint as a mum was a pretty shit one. I couldn't believe within months of moving to Newham I had become one of their pregnancy statistics and was convinced it was because of the move there (rather than my lack of contraception) that I had gotten pregnant. Where I'd normally have felt guilt about eating fast food, now I didn't, and indulged in cheap, hydrogenated fried chicken as I waited for the Big Day. Pregnant women got to eat what they wanted after all.

I felt like I was the only Asian in the history of Asians to get an abortion. I mean, white people didn't talk about these things, but shit, it wasn't even on the radar for Asians. If I didn't feel very Asian before this, I certainly felt a disqualified member by this point. What kind of Muslim would do this? And yet this was the only option I had. I could not look after a baby and there wasn't anything to be gained from keeping it. I didn't need to use it as collateral to keep the dad in my life. Ray J offered to come with me but given I didn't even want to be going myself I thought I'd spare him the ordeal. I always found it easier to tackle things on my own, rather than to let anyone in. He ended up going to his friend's father's funeral on the day. Chris also offered to come with me for support. Most of his clients would have him attend awards shows and the like, I couldn't have him come to this, though it meant a lot to be asked.

It was a morning appointment, and it was in Greenwich in South London. I presumed it was a non-local clinic so I wouldn't have to worry about being recognised. I was the first appointment of the day. I felt like such a hypocrite going into the clinic with my headscarf on. It was a reminder to me that I wasn't who I appeared to be – even though I was Muslim – I didn't deserve to be recognised as one for what I was about to do. But I wore it as I always did through the good and bad. I walked into the reception and gave my name. She gave me a form to complete. As I was the only one there, I stood by the counter, filling it in. I had the choice of two types of abortion: a vacuum abortion or one with pills. The doctor had recommended the former due to it being a smoother process. I opted for the latter because it seemed easier and less intrusive. It then came to next of kin and I drew a blank. I didn't have anyone to put. I couldn't put my parents as they didn't even know I wasn't a virgin. I thought about Ray J but that thought just made me laugh. I left the field blank and handed it back to the receptionist. She looked at me blankly and told me to make my way to the waiting area.

I sat down next to a plant in the corner. The magazines were old. I pretended to read them but all I was doing was flicking through them, I just needed to give my hands something to do. I felt so uncomfortable and awkward. It felt like I was doing something wrong. Eventually my name was called into room one. The nurse smiled at me, she was a Black lady and her kindly face and straight-talking imparted a confidence in me that she had done this before and was safe hands to be in. She did a scan of the baby. It was hiding near my right pelvic bone. She nodded her head and the corner of her mouth lifted as she finally located it on the screen. Before it had all been in my mind, but when she rubbed the gel on my stomach and moved the sonogram around, it felt real. I was sad to have to be doing this. A part of me really didn't want to. A baby was a gift from God. Not only would killing it be morally reprehensible but in the back of my mind I knew I would be unleashing a whole can of bad karma upon myself, both in this world and the next. Back at the nurses' desk she took some tests and asked me if I was sure I wanted to do this and said that counselling was available if I wasn't. My mind said no, I wasn't sure, and wondered if there was a third option that didn't involve aborting or having the baby. But I had been raised to go through the motions and so I said yes, I was sure, before signing a piece of paper to that effect.

I was asked to go back and wait in the waiting room. It had gotten busier. There was a super-slim white lady there – so thin I couldn't believe she was pregnant. I think I had gotten carried away with eating for two. Although she had just gone in to see the doctor, she ended up leaving before me. You never knew what happened in that tiny room. Whether someone had changed their mind or not. Then there was another white couple. At least the guy had come along with her. They were there with a small child in a pram and another toddler on the loose. I mean, fancy bringing kids along to an abortion clinic – what an advert for an abortion. This did bring a brief smile to my face as it felt completely ridiculous. The poor kids didn't have a clue where they were. The nurse called me back and said that due to my blood type they had to give me a precautionary injection. She assured me that abortion was a completely normal thing but suggested I considered contraception in future. She said she had had the same lady back there five times and while they were there to help, they didn't encourage abortions to be used as a contraceptive. I gave her a sincere nod – promising to comply – if she could just help me out with the pills. Sadly, I always swore to change and learn from something when it was too late.

I was asked back into the room and after taking some pills orally was told to insert four pills up my vagina. I had never fingered myself before and this felt like a terrible way to start. I barely let a guy finger me, it just wasn't something that I enjoyed. I did think a guy inserting the pills would have been much more fun than doing it myself. But I had got myself into this mess and

I would need to do this to move forward. And that's what I did. I inserted all four inside. Was it right? Was it wrong? – I didn't know. And I asked the nurse if she wanted to check they were properly inserted but she seemed confident they were without looking. This really hit home how poorly I knew my vagina. The nurse gave me sickness pills and told me I would need painkillers as it would hurt. She reminded me to eat with them and that the termination should take place within a few hours, but the timeline could vary. As I said bye, she comforted me by saying that no one needed to know.

I made the long journey home on public transport. I never felt enough self-worth to grab a taxi. Not even here and now. I had agonised if there had been some way to spare the baby and take me instead, but they haven't invented a way to do that yet. I felt fine most of the journey back but started to get a bad tummy ache a few minutes from home. As soon as I got home, I logged back into work. At the time I was a complaints manager for a bank and had managed to get the morning off by saying I had a doctor's appointment. I worked and waited for death. I hadn't missed anything at work, but I had been conscious of all the flexibility they'd granted at short notice for when I would go and do comedy jobs, and so I felt that I had to return the loyalty.

By 4 p.m. there was no sign of blood. I rang up the abortion aftercare line at 5 p.m.

'Hi, um, I had my appointment this morning at 10

a.m. and there hasn't been any bleeding. The lady at the clinic said I should start officially losing the baby roughly two hours after taking the pills.' I didn't add that when I'd got home, I'd noticed that one of the pills had dislodged. I was worried that maybe due to this the procedure might not have worked. Mild googling showed there's a very small fraction of abortions, like one per cent, that are unsuccessful. Maybe the baby wouldn't take no for an answer. If so, it'd be easier for some outside entity to make that determination instead of me.

I was confused and tired at this point. I'd taken an array of eighteen different pills that the nurse had pre-scribed, and it was all so draining. Having an unwanted body within my own unwanted body.

The nurse on the phone heard me but reeled off, 'It can take up to twenty-four hours after the procedure to lose the baby. If there's no sign within twenty-four hours, then you should call us back.' I couldn't see that in the mini booklet that had been handed to me, but I just took the advice I was given.

I started to lose the baby at 8.30 p.m. that night.

I texted Ray J. I told him it had been so hard when she did the scan.

He texted back:

It's just a blob of cells. No one has to know, it's the modern day, no one will think any less of you.

If no one knew, then of course they wouldn't think any less of me, but I was still in shock and I had to deal with the feelings it brought up. He was completely missing the point. For once it was about *me*. It was about how I felt and what I thought about it. Up until then, I had thought of sex bombs as being a bombshell; someone that was sexually undeniable. And in my case, I thought it was my dick jokes and my sex-related comedy and openness about it. This, however, was my sex bomb. A cocktail of bad decisions, not loving myself and making a huge mistake.

I felt completely numb by the entire course of events. Ray J wanted sex and came knocking on my door a few weeks later. The abortion hadn't been a big deal to him. But apparently, I was fertile right after an abortion and, as much as I needed sex (or probably more companionship and closeness), I didn't want to risk going through that all over again. I remembered what the lady had said about the five-abortions woman. I suppose having one showed I was human, but it wasn't a character trait I was looking to develop.

A few months later, I had started to move on, although it was something I regretted as it could so easily have been avoided by taking precautions.

I know Muslim women would have had abortions before me, I can't have been the only one, even if I felt like that was the case at the time. I wonder how many other Muslim or Asian women had experienced what I had or gone through their own sex bomb with no one to talk to. We're taught nothing about sex. Nothing. We don't fully understand our sexuality. We're encouraged to ignore our emotions; go with our head rather than to give head. Without knowing that our sexuality is ours to control, it is easy for it to be used for and by others. I understand the need for modesty and to have self-respect, but we need to open ourselves up to the possibilities that these things could and are happening to a number of us. Sexuality is part of being human and Muslim woman are no angels. Muslim women are fucking. We have been fucking for time and nobody talks about it. We're often fucking Muslim men whose judgement will come for us when they are done fucking us. They can't fuck us and judge us at the same time! I wonder if having to live up to such an unattainable saint-like image was setting me up to fail. Sex is a currency in many ways, so without knowing how to use it Muslim women run the real risk of being short-changed.

I'm a lot more careful now during sex. I don't wonder what it would have been like if I had kept it, there's no use. I already know it would be a completely different world to the one I'm living now. I don't think it'd be bad. It just wasn't the right life for me.

28

Portrait of a Lady on Fire

My community sometimes comments on what I
 wear.
They look at the scarf and they're like good girl.
They look at the rest and they're like, yeah she
 could do better.

It's not just them.
White guys sometimes come up to me and they're
 like 'You're a Muslim girl you shouldn't be
 wearing X.'
Always worried about what I'm wearing or what
 I'm not wearing, since when did you become
 so interested in fashion?
Especially considering White guys dress like they're
 builders out of the 1980s.

White guys are very specific about the hair they
  want to see as well.
Show me the hair on your head, but never have
  hair on your legs.
Go away and work on that, white guys.

Saying that, when it comes to dating the scarf has
  so many connotations I never signed up for.
The scarf says
I'm bad
I'm good
You're unclean
I'm a virgin
I could be corrupted.

People are like 'is it hot in the scarf?'
I'm like 'yeah, but not in the way you think.'

I was told by a firm feminist at the age of seventeen
that I was a feminist by default if I believed in equality
for men and women. It wasn't a choice, it was a movement, that if I wasn't a part of, I would be steamrolled
by. She was preying on young people's impressionable
fears, to feel a part of something, though it felt innocent enough. I've realised since that it's a little more
complicated than that, and a hundred times over since.
See, what I didn't realise at the time was that I did have
a choice and that choice being taken away from me

wasn't right, it was probably against what the essence of the movement stood for. I know a subsection of white people that would consider me or my ethnicity or my culture backwards. For we understand that men have certain responsibilities that differ from those of women, like putting food on the table. Their contributions to one another, the household, are equal but not the same. As someone who didn't come from the most stable of starts in life, the idea of clearly defined structures and roles which could of course be malleable, as and when required, was somewhat soothing to me. While modern feminism would frown at the idea that there is such a thing as a 'woman's place', this isn't something that phased me, for I also had certain expectations from men. It's not to say that the advancement of women's rights hasn't achieved milestones or made so many more opportunities for women around the world a possibility, far easier than ever imagined, but it is at least to acknowledge that this came at a price.

While the impact of the patriarchy arguably affected women in similar ways, mainstream white feminism in no way allows for the differences in women's relationships and attitudes towards the patriarchy. It was all very black and white: patriarchy bad, down with the patriarchy. But so many Asian households honour these same men and so this approach feels at odds with the very foundations that our families are built upon. As such, mainstream feminism is incompatible with quite significant elements of Asian culture and Asian culture with this feminism. It was of course so much more than just to do with gender. White feminism isn't compatible with Asian values a lot of the time, which means changes or compromises are required at both ends of the spectrum, in ways that white women aren't required to undertake or willing to accept.

Rather than be headhunted into feminism, like it was the Jehovah's Witness programme, I would have preferred to have had the space to explore what feminism meant to me. I was led to believe it is the same for every woman, but that simply isn't feasible given the extraordinary differences in our experiences and our histories. Although at times I tried to impersonate a good feminist, for the greater good, it felt like being a performative coconut*, as rather than being myself it felt as though I was doing a caricature of a white woman. I did this at times to fit in, to make myself amenable to others, quite often in the workplace where people felt uncomfortable around Muslim women. It was so far removed from what I recognised as the way Asian aunties and females would speak, I could hardly even take myself seriously. How could I fight for rights when I didn't even have any understanding of what my rights were? Feminism looked different on a white person than it did on a Brown person. On

---

* An ethnic person known to be trying too hard with white people.

a white person it was a cool 'cause', even charitable. On a Brown person it exemplified assimilation or even a struggle with oppression. It gave a pressure of something to live up to and I think as women and people we already had enough pressure to live up to. As a multiple card-carrying woman, I loathed to have to carry any more labels. I was already Asian, Muslim, Hijabi – I personally did not need any further groups to join. I was crying out to explore who I was and not be a spokesperson for the sum of my parts. I didn't see being a woman as being a victim, despite the impression feminism left.

To the patriarchy I was disobedient and 'too modern', and to feminists I was too submissive. I was neither a feminist nor traditional enough to be considered a patron of the patriarchy. For me, feminism makes it difficult to get to the truth: that power was and always has been up for grabs. It was up to you to grab it. At times feminism seemed as though it was a barney between white men and women – again something I didn't really have any direct concern with. Not to sound like an awful ally, but lol white women didn't need me as an ally. Although superficially it looked nice to have a Brown face in the mix, there was a sense that it was better that I was seen and not heard as it could be disruptive. On a human level, I couldn't help but be disappointed at times when rather than try and achieve progress, these two heavyweights would rather have a public go-to for all to see – completely ignorant of the wider ramifications. While I am sure they would have convinced themselves that in doing so this was to somehow uphold feminism, I doubt sparring online with, at times, well-meaning strangers is what the suffragettes would have indulged in. Which brings me to my biggest issue with feminism in its current format: internet feminism.

The movement online largely consists of feminist 'do-gooders' that want the appearance of being an activist but more by way of achieving social capital. In other words, it is privileged people amassing more privilege by arguing they are in fact underprivileged. Rather than uplifting those less privileged, they have a habit of speaking on their behalf. It is a way of getting attention and saying the right thing, even appearing popular and relevant, without really achieving very much for the movement at all, certainly not intentionally. It is hard therefore to discern the genuine feminists from the ones having bi-weekly online meltdowns. For me it is all talk, the performance is empty, and though it still might have on occasion achieved its goals (in spite of itself) by generating awareness or traction – it has sort of lost itself. We are all on different points of our own journeys and understandings, and while the universal principles of feminism feel harmless enough, as someone who isn't a middle-class white woman, it is asking considerably more of me. I would have to question everything as an Asian woman and (in its current format) possibly run the risk of alienating those around me to whom the ideology had failed to persuade.

As many Asian women are already caretakers of their families from an early age, it feels like a lot to expect us to take on the additional burden of reshaping the family – as well as go to school and try and have a semblance of a life, in part to appease the white woman or the status quo. It feels at odds that while our contribution would be bigger our representation would be tokenistic. Though earlier waves of feminism have facilitated the means with which women operate today, it is a huge question as to what the current phase has set out to achieve. This is important to know, particularly as ethnic women we would have more to lose as we are far more closely aligned and dependent upon men. Would we also be last in line to reap the benefits? The movement isn't transparent about intersectionality and still hasn't figured out how to be inclusive, for that would mean changing at its core.*

In some respects, it feels as though we've gone from

---

* Some of the most prominent feminists today are the worst adverts for the movement. They see through women like me, all the while feigning deep concern for my 'plight' which they really have no concept of – it is usually an elaborate ploy to show they are capable of having 'compassion'. It feels as though feminism has gotten so big it has lost the ability to be self-aware/critical.

having some responsibilities to many more responsibilities, therefore leading us to spread ourselves more thinly across the board. I get that it shouldn't be taken for granted what a woman's place is, but by us being a jack of all trades, as we are now, it sometimes makes it harder to enjoy the fruits of being a woman. With feminism being a tour de force as soon as I left my teens, as a working-class girl I never got to enjoy a gentleman pulling out a chair for me to sit down on or holding a door open or even buying me a bunch of flowers. OK, so maybe they've opened a door for me, but it wasn't by someone who I was going to shag which would have been decidedly more exciting. The thing is, equal is not equitable, and feminism has made men complacent in thinking that everything should be equal, and they shouldn't have to do these things. But to be equitable they should be doing them, to make up for the strain the patriarchy puts on women. They should be easing the weight, not having responsibility taken off them because women are simply working a lot harder.

Feminism largely achieved the majority of what it set out to well before I got here. It doesn't feel as though the later stages were as impactful. I shouldn't be required to be indebted to it for the rest of my life, particularly as its legacy largely criticises the choices of women from my background. It's dangerous of groups or movements to try and conveniently pass off our differences, such as access to resources and standards of living, with broad generalisations. While it wasn't ever emphasised that it was just a white woman's movement, it seems so obvious to me that that's what it was, given the people who started it and then continued to use it as a means to talk down to others, which is perhaps why such a disclaimer isn't ever necessary. It is the same reason white women are never expected to assimilate, whereas Asian and Black people are by default.

While it is refreshing to see women take the platform – what I didn't recognise is these same women being so unable to be vulnerable.* It is all 'girl power' and women 'on the frontline', which is progress, but at the same time real equality to me is also not having to be these things. It should just as much have been about being able to get a guy to open a pickle jar. This doesn't mean I am wholly repressed or doomed to live a life as a second-class citizen – it just means that I want the pickles! I don't need men to overlook me as a person to feel more of a woman. I wanted to feel like a woman. The way feminism seems to be promoted online or to people like me who didn't subscribe to it, is that there is an unspoken expectation for women

---

* Contrary to perception, the majority of ethnic women are actually too accustomed to independence. We need to open ourselves up to the possibility of love and being cared about.

to 'man up' which isn't really about women at all. For all the women it had helped empower, I sometimes think of the others that it has shamed into silence. The women who are happy being wives, stay-at-home mums, doing the cooking and housework. This isn't any less than the women who want it all, in my eyes – however not according to feminism.

There is nothing to be ashamed of in being nurtured, and not constantly being the one who nurtures others, in seeking security, in being a little weak sometimes. Though thanks to radical feminists this is no longer a tolerable means by which to view women these days. I'd like to see us individually apply our own definitions of womanhood rather than feeling as though we have to match up to some arbitrary, undefined expectation of what a 'modern woman' should be, or one that is moulded in a more masculine identity. With so much of what being a woman resembles being defined by white women, can you really blame me for not identifying with yet another movement that they front with very little thought of how it affects women like me? Frustratingly, the movement does nothing to help me or Muslim women be seen (or heard) for who we are, but rather it creates a division between us and more privileged women who automatically assume we are repressed and in need of 'saving'. These women to me are as toxic as the men they were at odds with, but for the life of them they can't see this for themselves.*

I am supposed to be upset with men speaking on my behalf, but totally fine with privileged white women doing this? I had experienced this with Lucy a lot, where my lack of social standing was fetishised. It was infuriating to stand back and witness my disenfranchisement being reimagined by white women as collateral for their social justice initiatives – which excluded me – and quite badly at that. This was difficult to reconcile – on the one hand these women had the means, tenacity and, let's face it, the time to help, but even so, they are so busy talking about the change that nothing else happens. Regardless of this, relying on them doesn't feel like it correlates with me being an independent woman.

I question any movement that makes people who aren't subscribed to it feel lesser. At the time the message was 'women shouldn't be afraid to make the first move with men'. Given that lots of Muslim women, like me, had never even had a conversation or shaken a man's hand during their teens, this was a

---

* It's a very specific type of middle-class, well-to-do white women who see it as their place to do so. Sometimes they masqueraded it by giving an ethnic person a platform. It's not 'giving back' when returning something that already belongs to the person!

little steep.* There isn't just one way of doing things. I didn't want to ask a guy out. I could, I wasn't frightened or a wimp – I just wanted the honour of being asked! It was fair enough for these women to complain about wolf-whistling towards themselves but I'm not sure this gives them the right to speak for all women. Considering Asian freshies only wanted me for my British citizenship, a builder appreciating me for my body by throwing me a whistle was a step up and the most attention I would hope to get all year!

I wish I had been smart enough to really observe the people who benefit the most from feminism. To study its most prominent members and then consider why they are predominantly wealthy, often married, white women. I mean, there is an unspoken hypocrisy that goes hand in hand with them dissuading others from being happily settled/coexisting with men, when that's what they would have for themselves. If I had this insight on 'the way things are' it would have been clear enough to me that this is not an inclusive movement for all, but an exclusive one for an esteemed few. This isn't wrong, but pretending to be something other than this is. It is an indirect way of trying to align women's politics, without us even knowing it. Some feminists

---

* It is harder for me as an Asian girl as I couldn't hide behind drunken texts or twirl my hair (though I did twirl my hijab once). I am expected and compelled to be in my senses all of the time.

I've encountered have some of the most impeccable characters of anyone I've ever met, but I put this down to them being great people rather than the wonders of feminism.

My biggest regret is that feminism took away some of my innocence which I'll never get back. This is because it implied inclusivity, and so I was all in until I realised that it was not for me at all as it unceremoniously left Muslim women in burkinis on the beaches in France in 2016 high and dry.* A lot of the shaming I received for 'not being sexy' is from white women. One person tweeted, in reference to my layers of clothing, 'Look at the state of you.' There is a sense from these women I was stuck in prehistoric times, rather than an acceptance of the differences in how women present themselves.

The reality is no one could be feminist all of the time, particularly if you're a woman, it just isn't practical while trying to keep your head above water. If it had taught me anything about my autonomy rather than invoking a blind allegiance, I would have far more respect for it than I do.

---

* France issued fines/penalties to Muslim women for wearing burkinis at the beaches during the infamous 'burkini' ban.

**Things I enjoy about men that would make
a token feminist shriek into a pillow:**

♡ Guys carrying my bags.

♡ Guys paying for things – dinner, lingerie and
my gym membership.

♡ Guys fixing stuff that's broken and being in
charge of DIY.

♡ Guys giving me their seat.

♡ Guys noticing the effort I've gone to (or not)
and paying me a compliment.

♡ A cheeky wolf-whistle.

♡ A guy working on cars and taking them to
the garage.

♡ Guys chopping logs for the fire.

29

Sister Act

A comedian asked me to perform comedy at a sex positivity event in Vauxhall to a crowd of about a hundred people. It was unpaid. It was an all-Muslim line-up during Ramadan, so I said sure and thought nothing else of it. Except it was a gig that was organised by someone who works in PR, and she wanted to generate lots of press for the night. She asked the group of acts if any of us fancied writing a feature in the *Metro* to promote the night. I offered and she put me in touch with the editor. I was between romantic options* at that point as I was really focused on comedy. I was offered voluntary redundancy at work – as they

---

* Sexual.

were outsourcing jobs to my cousins in India – and had accepted. This meant I could finally focus on comedy full time.

Being so busy performing meant my diary revolved around gigs and stage time which made it hard to hold down a steady relationship. Nevertheless, a girl could dream, and so I wrote an article about my experiences of sex as a Muslim woman. Quite frankly I loved having sex any time of the year and Ramadan is no exception. Rosy Edwards, my editor, had been very supportive in helping me draft and edit the piece. I knew they were running the piece to promote the gig, what I hadn't realised was, they were going to be publishing it to coincide with the beginning of Ramadan, the date of print Sunday 5 May 2019. They also added the title 'Horny Muslim women like me aren't supposed to exist during Ramadan.'

As soon as they posted the article online it blew up! People from outside my community welcomed the piece. There was also lots of support from members of my own community, but not everyone appreciated it. Here are some of the comments that I got on my Instagram post sharing the article:

Salam sis I hope you are doing well on this night leading to Ramadan. I just wanted to ask is it true that you believe in sex before marriage? The deen does state that sex before marriage is not allowed. Yes, we understand that sex is a fundamental part of our lives and that it's a healthy thing that married couples engage in within the tenets and within the fortress of marriage. As Muslims we have also been ordered to observe modesty not just in our hijab but in how we speak and interact with others. Just some advice from one sister to another, not claiming I'm perfect at all. May Allah bless you.

I don't know what went wrong but please don't see her as an inspiration. Even if you commit zina* you shouldn't brag about it or encourage others. Maybe Islamic rules will feel oppressing in this Western society but remember they protect us and are a test. Yes, you can live your life as you want but remember it will end so fast. I don't care what someone does but what you are doing is claiming to be Muslim, talking about Ramadan and spreading immorality so I had to say something. May God lead you all to the right path.

You talk about hooking up for casual sex with men during Ramadan, wanting dick from non-Muslim men etc, but that is a direct rejection of the tenets of the Quran and Prophet Muhammad pbuh. Also why would one deliberately seek to commit sin, as you state you would like to commit 'haram'?†

Serious and genuine question and I don't want to seem rude but what is it with you, someone who represents the hijab

---

* Zina means sex outside marriage.
† Forbidden.

and showing off your sins such as zina because frankly that's what I'm guessing you aren't married and do have sex. If you wanted to do that you might as well take it off because at the end of the day you represent the hijab and that's not what hijab is about.

Following the article's publication in the *Metro*, *The Sun* decided to do a botched version (without my permission) and released a similar article the next day. This was closely followed by *Sputnik Russia*. It became an awkward affair of watching people who got it defending me from the few that had some objections. There were quite a few comments of support from Muslim men who said they hoped I was OK. As a broadcaster I've been taught well that there's never any joy found in any comments sections, as such it's a rule I have not to reply. Particularly as very few differences are ever resolved online. I recognised the responses from people who didn't understand where I was coming from. It was so unfamiliar to everything they are used to expect from visibly dressed Muslims.

It is impossible to live up to everyone's expectations when it comes to the hijab. It is easy to suggest that I should find a husband and get on with it – but what about the girls like me who were yet to find one? What about the girls for whom the fairy tale didn't go as planned? Were we meant to remain silently outcast?

The possibility, and reality, of Muslim women having

sex was something that I felt needed to be said. While it may have offended them for appearing to glorify pre-marital sex, it was more of a case of acknowledging the ways in which Muslim women were not depicted, or appreciated, as rounded or unique. It wasn't encouraging others to be salacious, I just wanted to put sex on the table for discussion.* What I was really rallying against is the accepted norm of embracing suffering in silence in a way that I had found was unsustainable for me. This wilful and enduring misery is a cataclysmic, unending ordeal that I could not in good faith promote. I wouldn't have this treatment unto others, so how could I deem this OK for myself?

As a woman of colour, I am not only judged for who I am but for who I'm not. After years experiencing ups and downs (with a lot more downs) in my life, I wanted to speak out for those who are different and not perfect, in the hope they might feel less alone. From my family structures to my journey with comedy, from my dating of men both good and bad to going through an abortion, I wanted to be honest and open about it all. Life's too short not to have the conversation and hopefully someone could learn from some of the mistakes I've made. After the articles, a few Muslim acts had pulled

---

* Although it was early on in Ramadan, the first fast can be pretty tough and it was difficult to discern between the angry and the hungry commentators.

out of the gig at the last minute. They were concerned about their image and that the backlash might affect their earnings and future gigs/work.

I broke my fast at sunset at the venue with a glass of water and headlined the show.

There are a lot more similarities between Islam and comedy than I had anticipated. They both made something out of misery. In comedy, there is joy to be had from my sadness. In Islam, the more hardships I have, the more character building it is and could open doors in the hereafter. They both hold true that good could come from pain; whether that is in the form of a lesson or a laugh, it is some comfort to know that it isn't all in vain. As challenging as comedy is, it is a wonder that I didn't call it quits when every sign was telling me I should. I stuck with it because I didn't use my head but my heart, and though it packs punches, what doesn't kill you makes you stronger. It gives me an outlet to be more than the sum of my parts or the Muslim representative that people have me down as. No one *ever* took me seriously my whole life and then I picked an occupation where that's basically the job description! But I learnt there's a difference between making a sacrifice and being a sacrifice.

Islam said I was special. Hijabis would often be the subject of inspirational quotes such as 'Muslim women are the diamonds of Islam. Nobody will reveal their diamonds to strangers.' People in comedy, in turn, were quick to affirm how special a talent I am. In both cases, being special, rather than helping me, was a reason for holding me back. I felt anything but special. I voluntarily relinquished the title, not feeling worthy of such reverence and also out of wanting to be true to who I am. That was met with condemnation too. As though I should have been grateful to live up to preconceptions of me as opposed to defining them for myself. It's very risky to walk alone, without being affiliated, and that's something I hadn't fully thought through. I would have got a lot further along by playing the game and being the version of me that people wanted so much to see.

I know I was right to challenge the norms of being an Asian woman by not having an arranged marriage when this wasn't what I wanted. But I wish I had backed that up by being more confident and being empowered in having a plan to find another way, so that I believed I am worthy of love, and not just sex. Love is a drug and you need to be careful who you choose to be your dealer. As a Muslim woman, I felt so desexualised that I compensated on that front, but in doing so let the other stuff, the *important* stuff, slide. Sexy is a feeling, not the way people perceive you. Sexy is how confident and happy you feel in yourself, and that's what makes a true sex bomb.

In the end, no one's approval matters, as the secret to both comedy and sex was in enjoying it. Although people initially didn't know how to process a Muslim with sexual wanton, it worked once I owned it for me. Sex is easy; it's the rest of it that's hard. I would have enjoyed sex more if I was loved, but I wasn't. What I didn't know was that that journey starts with me loving myself enough first. Although finding a good man's love is something to treasure, I now know that there is more than that. I've always been an Asian Babe, but now I'm an Asian Babe with self-understanding and self-love. I've learnt lessons the hard way, in the hopes it might help young women, especially Asian women, fully embrace themselves and all their complexities.

In 2012, after ten years in publication, *Asian Babes* ceased trading. But you only have to take a look around to see that there's more of us around than ever creating our own narratives. We're on mainstream magazines now, on your TV, in films and in all sorts of different jobs and careers. It's so easy to put women in boxes, judging whether we're the right or the wrong sort of girl, trying to make our identities and facets work for your head and understanding of the world, but ultimately, you can take the hijab off the girl, but you can't take the girl out of the hijab.

Writing this, Ray J texts:

> How's the book coming along? Better let me read that shit before it goes out.

Peace.

Acknowledgements

Thank you, God Almighty, Most High, for all Your blessings.

Katie Packer!!! All love and gratitude to you for making this happen. I am hugely thankful for all of your time, energy and for just getting it from the start. There are few like you, the world is truly blessed because of you. This book would not have been written if you hadn't believed in it. You worked tirelessly (through a pandemic) to make it so and it is due to your instinct and soul that this book has got to see the light of day. I'm so endlessly thankful to you for being so patient and thoughtful. Thank you for working with me, it has been a complete honour.

Thanks to my mum for everything you have taught me, and for being your amazing self.

Thank you to Motunrayo Onanuga for being such a true friend and always listening and believing in me. You are a blessing, and I am so lucky to have you in my life. You have been so strong for me and I will always appreciate your kindness and generosity; I love you. Also, a big shout out to Abiola, Ayomi and the whole family. You are everything a family should be.

Thank you to Rosy Edwards for absolutely everything. I wouldn't have been able to do this without your unreserved kindness and love. You are one of the best people I know. Your mentorship and editorial support from 'that' *Metro* article to this book has been incredible. I'm so grateful for you letting me be messy, for being understanding and listening when it was hard. The moment you said I could text you any time of the day or night you made me feel like a writer. You made me feel human the times I didn't. You've been incredibly supportive and understanding throughout what has been a very involved journey. Thank you for helping me write the best version of my first book.

Special thanks to Dr Guo Wen Zhao (Herb Zhao Chinese Medicine and Acupuncture, Hemel Hempstead) for your care, kindness and patience. I am deeply grateful for your wisdom and support.

Acknowledgements

Thank you to Eli Sessions at BBC Sounds for taking a chance on us, letting me and Monty take control of the airwaves. I loved making our podcast 'No Country for Young Women'. It was a huge opportunity and one that I have had so many takeaways from, particularly that as an Asian woman I did not know it all when it came to race! I will be eternally grateful to you for the opportunity and your unwavering support during the good and challenging times.

Of course, a shout-out to the fabulous team who also made it happen: my producers Lachlan Macara, Hannah Hufford and commissioner Andy Worrell! I'm sorry I made you call BBC Compliance so often!! Thanks for all your hard work and patience in working with us. It was a dream come true.

Thank you to my physio/sports massage therapist Jay Watson for being such a tirelessly amazing person. You've been there through the slim and the slim-thick years and always been so kind and supportive! I've learned so much from you about healing and the power of movement.

Thank you to Rosie Kendrick for your unreserved kindness and generosity in being a friend and mentor. You always show such deep understanding and have such rich character. You're so special – I'm so blessed to have your friendship. You have made such a huge difference to me, and it's like we've been friends forever.

Jon Brittain, thank you for reading an early version and giving me excellent notes and thoughts. You did so amid a lengthy third lockdown in a global pandemic no less. I loved every comment and you made the prospect of approaching the next draft a much easier one.

Thank you, Anna Morrison for designing the sexiest front cover.

Thank you, Sarah Shaffi, for your help editing. The book is in much better shape because of your great observations and input.

Thanks to Aruna Vasudevan for your remarkable edits and help with the book. Your comments really helped me immensely and have given it the polish it needed.

Big up the crew Jen McGee and Abby Kumar. Jen for always being honest and supportive and letting me borrow your Netflix. Abby, thanks for believing in me and always making me laugh.

Stu Laws, thank you for being the nicest person to work with in comedy. You have been such a good friend and I really appreciate all of the opportunities to work with you on your hilarious projects.

Love to Dr Davina Ledermann for always being such a great friend.

Thank you so much to Dr Katherine E. Brown for reading my first draft. I appreciate your thoughtful and insightful comments and all the work you do in academia. Thank you to Jena Friedman, Gus Beattie

Acknowledgements

(Gusman Productions), Miriam Williamson (BBC), Leanne Alie (BBC Sounds), Rebecca Mulraine and Ella and everyone at Amazing Productions, and Gurinder Chadha.

Thank you to my friends Sharon-Leigh Gordon and Akin Kolade.

Thanks to the BBC for your support from the beginning.

Love to Headline.

And to *you* – yes, you.*

I will always love you, Nadeem.

---

* Thank you so much for reading.

Resources

MIND

A mental health charity raising awareness and providing support and advice to anyone experiencing a mental health problem. Their website also contains a wealth of information about how to get help, your rights, sectioning, discrimination and more.

www.mind.org.uk

0300 123 3393

info@mind.org

SAMARITANS

Samaritans provide emotional support to anyone who is struggling, with specially trained volunteers available to listen by phone or over email, twenty-four hours a day, seven days a week.

www.samaritans.org

116 123

jo@samaritans.org

MUSLIM YOUTH HELPLINE

Faith and culturally sensitive support services for young people in the UK. They offer non-judgemental, confidential support seven days a week, all year round.

https://myh.org.uk

0808 808 2008

help@myh.org.uk

SEX ADDICTS ANONYMOUS

A group of people who share their experience, strength and hope with each other in order to find freedom from addictive sexual behaviours and help others recover from sex addiction.

info@saauk.info

SEX AND LOVE ADDICT ANONYMOUS

Open to anyone who knows or thinks they have a problem with sex addiction, love addiction, romantic obsession, co-dependent relationships, fantasy addiction and/or sexual, social and emotional anorexia.

   contact@slaauk.org

SEXAHOLICS ANONYMOUS

A group of men and women who share their experience, strength and hope with each other so that they may solve their common problem and help others to recover.

   24 hour helpline number 0300 111 7777

References

Prologue

https://en.wikipedia.org/wiki/Asian_Babes

Chapter One

https://en.wikipedia.org/wiki/Arranged_
marriage#:~:text=Arranged%20marriage%20is%20a%20
type,spouse%20for%20a%20young%20person.
http://news.bbc.co.uk/1/hi/uk/4669284.stm
https://dictionary.cambridge.org/dictionary/english/hijab
https://www.britannica.com/topic/Hadith
https://dictionary.cambridge.org/dictionary/english/dowry

References

Chapter Three

https://www.crufts.org.uk
   https://dictionary.cambridge.org/dictionary/english/fetishize
   https://dictionary.cambridge.org/dictionary/english/halal

Chapter Four

https://themuslimvibe.com/featured/sex-in-islam-the-benefits-and-etiquette-for-a-healthy-sex-life

Chapter Eight

https://dictionary.cambridge.org/dictionary/english/savannah

Chapter Thirteen

https://www.healthline.com/health/mental-health/stockholm-syndrome#:~:text=Stockholm%20syndrome%20is%20a%20psychological,years%20of%20captivity%20or%20abuse.

Chapter Fourteen

https://languages.oup.com/google-dictionary-en/pimping

Chapter Sixteen

https://www.collinsdictionary.com/dictionary/english/iftar

Chapter Eighteen

https://www.britannica.com/topic/code-switching

Chapter Twenty-Four

https://www.bbc.co.uk/programmes/p063zy3c/episodes/downloads

Chapter Twenty-Five

https://dictionary.cambridge.org/dictionary/english/polygamy
https://www.bbc.co.uk/bitesize/guides/zdxdqhv/revision/7

Chapter Twenty-Eight

https://dictionary.cambridge.org/dictionary/english/burkini